T0294480

A BEGUM
& A RANI

A BEGUM & A RANI

HAZRAT MAHAL *and* LAKSHMIBAI IN 1857

RUDRANGSHU MUKHERJEE

PENGUIN
ALLEN
LANE

An imprint of Penguin Random House

ALLEN LANE

USA | Canada | UK | Ireland | Australia
New Zealand | India | South Africa | China

Allen Lane is part of the Penguin Random House group of companies
whose addresses can be found at global.penguinrandomhouse.com

Published by Penguin Random House India Pvt. Ltd
4th Floor, Capital Tower 1, MG Road,
Gurugram 122 002, Haryana, India

First published in Allen Lane by Penguin Random House India 2021

Copyright © Rudrangshu Mukherjee 2021

ISBN 9780670090662

Typeset in Sabon by Manipal Technologies Limited, Manipal
Printed at Replika Press Pvt. Ltd, India

www.penguin.co.in

To the memory of two Lucknow personalities,
Ram Advani and Mohini Mangalik

'May these characters remain
When all is ruin once again.'

CONTENTS

Contents

LIST OF ABBREVIATIONS

- Cons.: Consultations
- For. Dept.: Foreign Department
- Forrest, *Selections: Selections from Letters, Despatches and State Papers in the Military Department of the Government of India, 1857–58*, 4 vols (Calcutta: Government of India: 1893–1912).
- *FSUP*: Rizvi, S.A., and Bhargava (ed.), *Freedom Struggle in Uttar Pradesh* (Lucknow: Publications Bureau: 1957; repr. Delhi: Oxford University Press: 2011).
- IOR: India Office Records in the British Library, London.
- Kaye: *Sepoy War*, Kaye, J.W., *History of the Sepoy War*, 3 vols (London: W.H. Allen: 1864–1876).
- NAI: National Archives of India, Delhi
- NWP: North-Western Provinces
- Proc.: Proceedings
- Sec/Secy: Secretary
- Suppl.: Supplement

INTRODUCTION

In Bertolt Brecht's play *The Life of Galileo*, there is a significant scene towards the end. It takes place on 22 June 1633 and is set in the palace of the Florentine ambassador in Rome. Galileo has been taken away to appear before the Inquisition. On stage are his three pupils, Andrea, Federzoni and the little monk—all eagerly waiting for news and hoping that Galileo will not recant his views. Also present is Virginia, the scientist's daughter, who is praying that her father will recant and thus not be damned. The announcement will be made by ringing the bells of St Mark's. The bells begin to toll, and the voice of the crier is heard saying that Galileo has renounced his belief in a heliocentric universe and has accepted the teachings of the Holy Church. The directions in the play read: 'The stage grows dark. When it grows light again the bell is still tolling, and then stops. Virginia has gone. Galileo's pupils are still there.' Andrea says loudly, 'Unhappy the land that has no heroes!' As he says this Galileo enters, 'completely altered by his trial,' Brecht writes, 'almost to the point of being unrecognizable. He has heard Andrea's last sentence. For a moment he pauses at the door for someone to greet him. As no one does, for his pupils shrink back from him, he goes slowly and unsteadily because of his failing eyesight, to the front [of the stage] where he finds a stool and sits down.' Brecht has Galileo say in response to Andrea, 'No. Unhappy the land that is in need of heroes.'[1]

Under British rule that followed military conquest, India was an unhappy land. The unhappiness of the common people was rooted in their poverty, which was a result of British exploitation. Among western-educated Indians, it stemmed from the realization that their past had been taken away from them, that British rulers had appropriated the Indian past. James Mill famously announced this act of appropriation in his book *The History of British India*, where he wrote, 'The subject [Indian history] forms an entire, and highly interesting, portion of the British history.'[2] The statement implied that India or Indians had no history before the arrival of the British. This effacement of the past also came with strains of disdain and condescension. Thomas Babington Macaulay wrote with supreme smugness: 'A single shelf of a good European library was worth the whole native literature of India and Arabia';[3] he heaped scorn on 'History, abounding with kings thirty feet high, and reigns thirty thousand years long—and Geography, made up of seas of treacle and seas of butter.'[4]

Western education brought to the new intelligentsia a new awareness of its own past. Colonial education—in institutions like Hindu/Presidency College in Calcutta or Elphinstone College in Bombay—had imparted lessons on the rational reconstruction of European history. However, when members of this intelligentsia turned to the history of their own country, they found that history to be written entirely from the British point of view. That past, in the writings of the British, carried a stigma: it was the tale of *kalanka*, of slander. Yet research by scholars associated with The Asiatic Society of Bengal pointed to an Indian past that was rich in philosophy, literature, political institutions and economic development. Sections of the western-educated literati, in the second half of the nineteenth century, took on the project of recovering the Indian past and freeing it from the biases and prejudices of British writers. This project was nothing less than an attempt to reconstruct an autonomous history of India. It was also informed by a sense of pride in one's own country and a sense of belonging. The writing of history became the domain where patriotism began to first assert itself—a 'pulling away,' in the words of Ranajit Guha, 'from servility, however feebly, towards an assertion of independence.' It was also an attempt to step out of the state of unhappiness to the state of pride in one's motherland.[5]

Given the state of history writing in the nineteenth century, it is not surprising that the attempt to represent India's past was based on individuals or what is often called the 'great man theory of history.' It is significant that the first three books on history to be published in Bengali were books based on individuals. Two of them—*Raja Pratapaditya Charitra* by Ramram Basu, published in 1801, and *Maharaj Krishnachandra Rayasya Charitram* by Rajiblochan Mukhopadhyay, in 1805— dealt directly with individuals. *Rajabali* by Mrityunjay Vidyalankar, published in 1808, was about the 'Rajas and Badshahs and Nawabs who have occupied the throne in Delhi and Bengal'.[6] Equally important to mention here is that one of the supreme achievements in the Bengali world of letters in the nineteenth century was Bankimchandra Chattopadhyay's essay 'Krishna Charitra' (1886)—a rather direct riposte to Macaulay's contempt for India's mythical past, which historicized the figure of Krishna as the exemplary modern individual.[7] India had its own history; the foreign rulers had obliterated it. That history had to be retrieved. The nineteenth century and the early twentieth century saw many such acts of historical retrieval in different parts of the country—all intellectual exercises to write an Indian history of India.

For the purposes of this book, none was more important than a short essay on the Rani of Jhansi published in 1877 by a sixteen-year-old Rabindranath Tagore, who was already making a name for himself in the literary world of Calcutta. Tagore began the essay, simply titled 'Jhansir Rani' (Rani of Jhansi)[8], by recalling the bravery of the Rajputs and the patriotism of the Marathas, which many believed had been extinguished under 1000 years of slavery. The history of the revolt of 1857 (Tagore called it *Sipahi Yuddha* or Sepoy War) had shown that such a conclusion was unwarranted. He wrote that the special virtues of these people had been asleep and subsequently woken up during the revolution. He drew attention especially to the courage and military achievements of Tantia Tope, Kunwar Singh and Rana Beni Madho of Sankarpur. If these and other heroes (*vira*) had been born in Europe, Tagore wrote, they would have been immortal in the pages of history, in the songs of poets, in sculptures and in monuments and memorials. However, in India, in the hands of British historians, the stories of these heroes were written in the most ungracious manner. Tagore added that these versions, too, would be washed away in time, and their lives would be unknown to future generations. Of the all the Indian heroes of 1857, Tagore drew special attention to one individual: 'the woman of valour (*virangana*), Rani Lakshmibai, the Queen of Jhansi, before whom we must bow our heads in reverence.' Tagore went on to depict her as the epitome of virtue: she was young, a few years over twenty, beautiful, strong in body and determined in her mind. She was endowed with a sharp intelligence and comprehended very well the complex issues of ruling and administration. British administrators, as was their wont, Tagore noted, had spread many canards about her character but historians had conceded that not a word of them was true. Tagore described how badly Lakshmibai had been treated by Lord Dalhousie. She had nurtured these grievances and when she heard that the *sipahi*s had mutinied, she prepared for vengeance. But Tagore was careful to point out that she had no hand in the massacre of the white population of Jhansi. There followed a description of Lakshmibai's defence of Jhansi against the British counter-insurgency onslaught, her escape from the city, her bravery in the battles at Kalpi and Gwalior, and her death while fighting.

Tagore admitted that his piece on the Rani of Jhansi was entirely based on British accounts. He had probably read John Kaye, whose three volumes were published between 1864 and 1876; in fact, his use of the phrase 'sipahi yuddha' is suggestive of his familiarity with Kaye's work, since 'Sepoy War' was how Kaye had described the events of 1857–58. Tagore may have also read Charles Ball's book *The History of the Indian Mutiny,* which was published in the 1860s— the first of the British narrative histories of the rebellion. Tagore's essay is among the first—if not the first account of Lakshmibai, as well as of any aspect of the 1857 uprising, by an Indian in any Indian language. The first history of the revolt in Bengali was to appear between 1879 and 1901;[9] the first volume was published two years after Tagore's essay. At the very end of his piece, Tagore wrote that his sketch of the life of the rani had been gleaned from the writings of British historians. He hoped to present in the future the history that he himself had gathered. There was thus a promise to write an autonomous—free of the contamination of British biases—history of the rani of Jhansi. That promise or agenda was not fulfilled.

That Tagore was the first to write about and to note that Lakshmibai deserved reverence and devotion (*bhakti*) is of some consequence for the argument that this book tries to make. The young Tagore unwittingly initiated a trend that has stayed on—to regard Lakshmibai as an object of devotion. Tagore was beginning the process of creating a national icon. Vinayak Damodar Savarkar, without knowing what Tagore had written, looked at Lakshmibai in the same vein. Similarly, in the 1920s, the famous poet and nationalist Subhadra Kumari Chauhan wrote a hymn to Lakshmibai in which she apotheosized the rani as an avatar of Durga. Her poem drew on the folklore of Bundelkhand and the songs of the *harbola*s of that region. In 1943, in South East Asia, Subhas Chandra Bose formed the Rani of Jhansi regiment and recruited young Indian women from Malaya and Burma (mostly but not exclusively Tamil) to join it. Bose, according to his biographer, cited Lakshmibai 'as a shining example of female heroism in India, comparable to France's Joan of Arc.'[10] Three years later, incarcerated at the Ahmednagar Fort, Jawaharlal Nehru sought emotional solace by recalling India's past. He wrote, with adulation, about Lakshmibai, who was to him 'the young heroine of the Indian Mutiny', and whose stories, like those of Akbar and Birbal, King Arthur and his knights, 'crowded into my mind'. It was the name of Lakshmibai that stood out above all the others who had fought in 1857—'it is still revered in popular memory', Nehru wrote.[11] India, the unhappy land, had created its heroine from the annals of the great rebellion.

As a kind of culmination of this iconization/lionization of Lakshmibai, on the occasion of the 150th anniversary of the revolt of 1857, Shubha Mudgal rendered Subhadra Kumari Chauhan's poem as a song in the Indian parliament to a packed house. Lakshmibai has thus become part of the nation's memory, a virangana in the national consciousness. She had always been a part of history but in the contest between Clio and Mnemosyne, the latter prevailed. How she was or is remembered has acquired greater importance than what actually happened in history. History is lost to memory and myth. She has been memorialized as national heritage. It is the duty of Indians to remember Lakshmibai over all the others who resisted and fought the British in 1857–58.

The act of remembering inevitably summons up its opposite or the Other—forgetting. The making of Lakshmibai into an iconic figure relegated, without anyone quite intending it, another woman rebel leader into relative oblivion. Hazrat Mahal, unlike Lakshmibai, was not a late entrant into the rebellion but had been a leader of the rebels in Awadh from the very beginning of the uprising. She continued in that role until late 1858, when, pursued by British troops, she was forced to flee to Nepal, where she died in obscurity. Hazrat Mahal made a brief and fleeting appearance in Tagore's essay on Lakshmibai. Describing the bravery of Rana Beni Madho, Tagore emphasized how Beni Madho had pledged his loyalty to the Begum of Awadh and Birjis Qadr and noted that Beni Madho had lived and died by that pledge. Exit Hazrat Mahal from Tagore's script. Savarkar, too, wrote of Hazrat Mahal's love of liberty and commitment to freedom but maintained that she was not quite up there with Lakshmibai. No poet wrote a song in praise of her. There is no evidence that Subhas Bose thought of raising a regiment in her name. And Nehru, when he discovered India, did not discover Hazrat Mahal. In his case, however, the forgetting of Hazrat Mahal takes on a different dimension. His baptism and subsequent radicalization in politics had occurred through his 'wanderings among the *kisans*' of Awadh in the early 1920s.[12] She stood forgotten in his recollections of many of the villages that he tramped around, addressing meetings and spending nights in locations where she had drawn popular support. Either the villagers who spoke to Nehru did not remember Hazrat Mahal, or what they said did not stick in Nehru's memory. Hazrat Mahal, it will not be unfair to assume, was not evoked by the peasants of Awadh in the way Lakshmibai was by the kisans and artisans of Jhansi and Bundelkhand. For the 150th anniversary of the uprising, Hazrat Mahala was scarcely commemorated. There was perhaps only a passing mention. Forgotten and unsung, Hazrat Mahal has travelled unclaimed in the luggage van of 1857.

One of the themes of this book is the important roles of Lakshmibai and Hazrat Mahal in leading the revolt in two different theatres of resistance. The first three chapters attempt to do this. Chapter 1 addresses the origins of the uprising and of these two individuals. Chapter 2 looks at the trajectories of the rebellion in Awadh and Jhansi and situates Hazrat Mahal and Lakshmibai in those tumultuous events.

The third chapter considers their different styles of leadership and how they mobilized people. In Chapter 4, I return to the theme of remembrance and forgetting by reflecting on the afterlife of the two women.

*

The annals of the revolt of 1857 are documented in the archives of the victors. However ironic that statement sounds, it is nonetheless true. Most of the rebels were too illiterate to leave behind written records. Any historian attempting to write the history of 1857 not from the perspective of the triumphant British but from the point of view of those who for a year and more challenged British rule—and in areas like Awadh and Jhansi successfully overthrew it for a few months—faces the problem of the absence of rebel voices and records. They are compelled to depend on the archives that the British created to record the success of their counter-insurgency operations. From the 'prose of counter-insurgency'—to use Ranajit Guha's phrase—it is possible to construct a history of insurgency. This method of reading the colonial archives against the grain has come to be associated with Guha, but it was first tried out by the historian S.B. Chaudhuri in a pioneering book on the revolt of 1857 published in the centenary year.[13] In this book, Chaudhuri was neither concerned with the British—their sufferings and their triumphs—nor with the sepoy mutinies that acted as a trigger to a more general revolt against British rule. He wanted to capture the activities of the rebels who were not sepoys but civilians. Setting out the purpose of his book, Chaudhuri wrote, 'The following pages . . . aim, so far as it is possible to bring within a convenient compass at presenting the history of the civil rebellion in the Indian mutinies in a connected and indisputably authentic form, its scope and character, the class of people participating in it, and the effect produced in the direction and dimension of this vast conflagration and in the prolongation of the conflict and its consequences . . . The leading object throughout has been to show, in its true proportion and colour . . . the relative share that the civil communities had in the conflict generally, and utmost care and research have been taken to draw from all sources any information tending to throw light on the part played and the influence exercised by the people of the countryside and other men of consequence in changing the course of the revolt from mutiny to rebellion.'[14]

The moot point, of course, was how Chaudhuri had reconstructed the activities of the rebels. He wrote that he had depended on government records, the narrative of events recorded by British district officers, parliamentary papers, reports, minutes of meetings, dispatches and memoranda preserved in what was then the Commonwealth Relations Office in London and the district collectorates of India.[15] (This entire archive is now housed in the British Library in the India Office Records section). In other words, Chaudhuri produced an account and analysis of the rebel activities entirely based on the archives of the victors. To justify this method, he wrote, 'No comprehensive account is available from the defeated side, but this limitation in a way enhances the authenticity of the records of the British officers who were compelled in accordance with official orders, to compile a narrative of the mutinies and to acknowledge the genuineness of the popular reaction to the sepoy war. There might have been wilful suppression of the details of the rebellious proceedings and a little inflation of the figures of the rebel forces to show the enormity of the danger they confronted, but the account of Indian rebellion furnished by the British themselves has at least this saving feature that it automatically rules out the charge of biased sources.'[16] The sources were obviously biased in favour of the British, and Chaudhuri demonstrated in great detail that it was possible from such sources to provide a narrative of how the rebels fought and how many of them were involved in the resistance to British rule. The colonialist archives could be prised open to reveal rebel activities.

Nearly three decades after Chaudhuri, the need to read the victors' archives to gain access to rebel consciousness was reformulated with greater sophistication by Guha, who asked, 'How . . . are we to get in touch with the consciousness of insurgency when our access to it is barred . . . by the discourse of counter-insurgency?' He answered the question with the following formulation, which has now become famous: 'The difficulty is perhaps less insurmountable than it seems at first sight. For counter-insurgency, which derives directly from insurgency and is determined by the latter in all that is essential to its form and articulation, can hardly afford a discourse that is not fully and compulsively involved with the rebel and his activities. It is of course true that the reports, despatches, minutes, judgments, laws, letters etc., in which policemen, soldiers, bureaucrats, landlords, usurers and others hostile to insurgency register their sentiments, amount to a representation of their will. But these documents do not get their content from that will alone, for the latter is predicated on another will—that of the insurgent. It should be possible therefore to read the presence of a rebel consciousness as a necessary and pervasive element within that body of evidence.'[17] In this book, following in the footsteps of Chaudhuri and Guha, I attempt to reconstruct the activities of the rebels in Awadh and Jhansi and the leadership provided by Lakshmibai and Hazrat Mahal from the records created and preserved by the British.

The statement made above, that rebel voices went completely unrecorded, because they were the voice of the defeated, is not entirely true. The counter-insurgency archive, for the reasons mentioned by Chaudhuri and Guha, contained quite a few proclamations or *ishtahar*s that the rebel leaders had issued. They articulated the grievances, aims and aspirations of the rebel leaders. Issued for the purposes of propaganda, persuasion and polemic, these proclamations recorded the authentic voice of the leadership. In Chapter 3 of this book, I look at some of this in detail to understand the kind of leadership that Hazrat Mahal and Lakshmibai aimed to provide. These ishtahars are the only direct access to the voice of the rebels. The archives recorded and preserved only these proclamations.

The unavoidable dependence on archives fashioned by the British produces a problem that is extremely relevant to this book and its argument. The British wrote fairly extensively about Lakshmibai—her bravery, her beauty, her pedigree, her death. Some writers (falsely) wrote about her perfidy and licentiousness. But the British did not write as extensively about Hazrat Mahal. In most British writings, she is a shadowy and fleeting presence. One reason for this was visibility. Lakshmibai had been seen by the British, most importantly on the battlefield fighting valiantly as a soldier. No such sighting of Hazrat Mahal was ever recorded. Her name occurs as someone who issued orders, planned troop deployment, held durbars, and sent out sharply worded proclamations, but she is never a physical presence. No one saw her on the battlefield. Abdul Halim Sharar, who wrote in the early twentieth century an account of life and culture in Lucknow, says, 'it was impossible for her [Hazrat Mahal] to discard her *purdah*.'[18] If this indeed were the case, it would explain why there is no available description of Hazrat Mahal's physical presence. With due deference to Sharar, it should be asked whether Hazrat Mahal was actually behind a purdah other than the few years that she was married to Wajid Ali Shah. She was the daughter of a slave, had trained in a music academy and had been a courtesan. It is difficult to believe that she had taken the purdah. During the uprising, she was on the move, especially when she escaped from Lucknow to the countryside in March 1858 before finally fleeing to Nepal. She could not have traversed hundreds of miles with a largish entourage in a purdah. The absence of Hazrat Mahal's physical appearance in the records thus remains something of a mystery. Lakshmibai was certainly much more prominent. This visibility of one and the invisibility of another left its imprint. This is unavoidable, no matter how one reads the documentation—with or against the grain. What the British wrote about Lakshmibai was echoed, although not in the same terms, by subsequent writers. What the documents make invisible cannot be rendered visible by historians. The historian's craft is perpetually haunted by the spectre of empiricism.

*

'Unhappy the land that is in need of heroes'—this evocative line can be contrasted and/or complemented by another equally poignant line from American poet May Sarton: 'One must think like a hero to behave like a merely decent human being.'[19] Lakshmibai and Hazrat Mahal went forth into battle not merely because one was a widowed rani and the other a discarded begum, but because they felt that they, their husbands and the people of Jhansi and Awadh had been treated unfairly and unjustly by a tyrannical and despotic government that was not willing to treat the rulers of the regions and their people as decent human beings. The rani and the begum joined tens of thousands of ordinary, decent human beings who had chosen to resist and overthrow an alien and oppressive political dispensation. It was their heroism and support that catapulted both these women into commanding positions. The memory of that leadership fashioned one into a legend and pushed the other into relative oblivion.

Resistance to tyranny is always a collective act, but unfortunately, there is a propensity to identify resistance with individuals and make them into heroes. We thus overlook other equally vital and vibrant aspects of resistance to tyrants.

ORIGINS

In 1857, the resistance of common people made leaders of obscure royals. It can be said without exaggeration or disrespect that neither Begum Hazrat Mahal nor Rani Lakshmibai would have made it to the pages of history had they not been drawn into the tumultuous events that enveloped north India in the summer of 1857. The latter was the queen of the small principality called Jhansi in Bundelkhand, in the south-western corner of present-day Uttar Pradesh (called the North-Western Provinces in the first half of the nineteenth century). Jhansi was annexed by the British in 1853. Hazrat Mahal was the discarded wife of Wajid Ali Shah, who, till the British annexed it in February 1856, had been King of Awadh, ruling it from Lucknow. Immediately after the annexation, Wajid Ali Shah was exiled to Calcutta. But Hazrat Mahal was left behind in Lucknow with her young son who was not yet in his teens. The lives of these women, who retained their titles, were poised to change due to events that unfolded far from Lucknow and Jhansi. Meerut, where the uprising began, was a small cantonment town north-east of Delhi, the capital of the Mughal Empire, where the old and powerless Mughal Emperor Bahadur Shah still lived.

In the late afternoon of 10 May 1857, the sepoys in Meerut broke out in open mutiny.[1] The trigger was something that had happened a few days earlier—a firing parade ordered by Colonel Carmichael-Smyth on 24 April. As soon as the order for the parade was posted, a discussion ensued in the sepoy lines. Two Muslim *naiks* or corporals, Pir Ali and Kudrat Ali, told their comrades that the new cartridges were greased with the fat of cows and pigs and would defile both Hindus and Muslims. The sepoys then took an oath—Muslims on the Quran and Hindus on the water of the Ganges river—that they would not use the cartridges until every regiment had agreed to do so. When the parade commenced, ninety sepoys of the 3rd Light Cavalry were asked to take the cartridges; eighty-five of them refused. The defiant men were taken off duty and confined to their lines. A court of inquiry that was later instituted recommended a court martial of all eighty-five men. The commander-in-chief approved the recommendation.

On 9 May, the punishment of the recalcitrant sepoys was organized as a spectacle. All the troops, British and native, were brought to the European infantry parade ground and made to form three sides of a square. The European troops were fully armed, but the sepoys were not. The condemned men were then marched into the square. The sentence was read out to them, they were stripped of their uniform and were then publicly chained. The last process—the shackling of the men—took over two hours. The condemned sepoys erupted in outcry. They taunted the other sepoys and appealed for rescue. As they were marched off to jail, they abused their

2

officers, especially Carmichael-Smyth, at whom some even hurled their boots. The ceremony of punishment imposed a palpable nervous strain on the native troops.

The outbreak of the mutiny the following day was not exactly unannounced. On the evening of 9 May, a native officer of the 3rd Light Cavalry visited Lieutenant Gough, the temporary troop commander at the time, to apprise him of the imminent mutiny in Meerut. Gough relayed this information to Carmichael-Smyth and Brigadier Archdale Wilson, both of whom dismissed it. The Meerut commissioner's wife, Mrs Greathed, told Colonel Custance of the Carabiniers that she had heard that placards calling upon all true Muslims to rise and slaughter the English had been put out in the city. Inquiries into the Meerut outbreak revealed that on the afternoon of 10 May, around 2 p.m., a sepoy had told a sex worker at Sadar Bazaar that the native troops were going to rebel that day. Even those who took these warnings seriously did not quite expect the ferocity of what followed.

It is difficult, of course, to pinpoint when and how the mutiny began. From all existing accounts, it seems that in the late afternoon, around 5 p.m., there was an outcry at Sadar Bazaar that European troops were coming to take away the arms and ammunition of the native regiments. The sepoys who were in the bazaar rushed back to their lines. Those of the 20th Native Infantry rushed forward to the bell of arms, broke it open and opened fire. They shot and killed Colonel Finnis. The 11th Native Infantry was also in uproar. A similar scenario unfolded in the cavalry lines. There, since the sepoys had horses, the action was swifter and the destruction more far-reaching. The sepoys from the cavalry rushed from the parade ground to the jail where their comrades had been sent the previous day. They broke open the jail and their incarcerated colleagues were freed. As a group of sepoys from the cavalry passed through the city, they called on the passers-by to join them in a war of religion.

In both the infantry and cavalry lines pandemonium reigned supreme, with sounds of gunfire all around. The soldiers set the lines and the bungalows on fire. One eyewitness recalled the scene: '. . . the lines were being burnt and there was a general rush to the magazine, where the men helped themselves to the ammunition—regardless of it being the "unclean cartridges". As for any efforts on my part to bring them to a sense of their duties or of obedience to my orders they were absolutely useless . . . After a time, the disregard of my authority changed to open mutiny; there were loud shouts of "*Maro! Maro!* (Kill him! Kill him!)" and a few men, chiefly recruits, fired pistol shots at me, mostly at random . . . [I] left at a gallop being for a time pursued with shouts and execrations.'[2]

The mutiny did not remain one for very long. It became an outbreak as the defiance and the violence moved from the barracks to the bazaar. As the news spread, crowds of ordinary people of Meerut, especially those belonging to the lower castes—'the bazaar mobs' according to British observers—joined the outbreak and charged into the bungalow area. Plunder, arson and murder followed. The targets were clearly defined: Europeans, all that the Europeans owned and the symbols of European power. Thus the bungalows were the first to be burnt, and the Europeans found in them or trying to escape were killed. Gender and age were no bar to the killings. The Old Jail, different from the one that the cavalry sepoys had stormed to free their comrades earlier, was broken into and the convicts were released. Sometime during the night, bands of villagers poured in from surrounding villages, further strengthening the rebels. The mutiny was poised to become a general uprising as the destruction was no longer limited to the hands of a disgruntled soldiery. Sepoys and civilians came together in an open rebellion. It is easy to assume that the destruction and violence were mindless and that the plunder was the product of greed. Such an assessment overlooks one simple but significant fact: sometime during the evening, as mayhem raged in Meerut, the rebels cut the telegraph line—the symbol of British rule and an alien way of life—to Delhi and Agra, which was also the quickest way to communicate news and ask for reinforcements. By doing so, the rebels ensured that their next object of attack could not be revealed. As night fell on Meerut, a group of sepoys sped southwards to Delhi, the seat of the Mughal Emperor.[3]

The sepoys from Meerut arrived at Lal Qila, the seat of the Mughal Emperor, Bahadur Shah II, early in the morning of 11 May. The palace was already awake as it was the month of Ramazan. Bahadur Shah was an emperor merely in name. His powers had been taken away from him by the British and he lived off a pension the British provided. He took refuge in music and poetry. Yet he enjoyed the charisma associated with the name of the Mughal Badshah.

The mutineers from Meerut entered the Mughal capital through the eastern end, crossing the Jamuna by the bridge-of-boats, where they killed the toll-keeper. The toll-house was set on fire and a European civilian who had driven up to the bridge was shot. Having crossed the river, the sepoys came to the eastern wall of the fort. It was here that Bahadur Shah saw them. He summoned his physician

5

Hakim Ahsanullah Khan and told him, 'Look, the cavalry are coming in by the road of the Zer Jharokha.' The sepoys rode up beneath the windows of the king's apartments and appealed to him, '*Dohai Badshah* (Help O King), we pray for assistance in our fight for the faith.' The powerless monarch, taken aback by this appeal, was in no position to respond and so he sent for Captain Douglas, the commandant of the palace guard. Douglas ordered the sepoys to go away. The sepoys moved off and Douglas got busy trying to close all the gates of the walled city. He was too late. Another group of sepoys from Meerut had already entered the city and begun plundering the European quarters in Dariyaganj. The sepoys soon started attacking and killing any European that they saw. The 38th Native Infantry on guard at the palace showed their defiance by refusing to close the palace gates and by firing their guns in the courtyard of Diwan-i-Khas. This prompted the king to step out and meet them. Ghulam Abbas, the vakil of the emperor, recalled the encounter: '. . . The officers of the cavalry came forward, mounted as they were, and explained that they had been required to bite cartridges, the use of which deprived both Hindus and Mahomedans of their religion, as the cartridges were greased with beef and pork fat, that they accordingly killed the Europeans at Meerut, and had come to claim his protection.' The King replied, 'I did not call for you, you have acted very wickedly.' Hearing this, about 100 to 200 of the mutinous infantry, the infantry from Meerut having also arrived by this time, ascended the steps and barged into the hall, saying, 'Unless you, the King, join us, we are all dead men, and we must in that case just do what we can for ourselves.' The King then seated himself in a chair, and the soldiery, officers and all, came forward one by one and bowed their heads before him, asking him to place his hand on them. The King did so, and each withdrew.[4]

An old and powerless monarch, surrounded by insurgents, reluctantly accepted the nominal leadership of the rebellion and gave it his blessing. A mutiny that had begun in Meerut had acquired the sanction and stamp of authority that was distinct from the British. It had acquired legitimacy.

Outside the Red Fort, in the city, the insurgency did not wait for any official sanction. The mutineers, joined by the common people of Delhi, proceeded to plunder, destroy and kill. The violence was directed at all things British and at Britons. The city and its populace went over to the rebellion. The Britons who survived took refuge on the Ridge, two miles north of the city.

The fall of Delhi had a remarkable impact on the cantonments all over north India. Between 10 May and 14 May, there were no outbreaks of violence. But once the news of the fall of Delhi travelled down the Ganges valley, the garrisons of north India raised the flag of revolt. The fall of Delhi was interpreted as the breakdown of British authority. As early as the end of the month, Henry Lawrence in Lucknow perceived the importance of Delhi in the way events were unfolding. He wrote to the secretary of the Governor General: 'Tranquillity cannot be much longer maintained unless Delhi is speedily captured.'[5]

Most historians of the revolt of 1857 tend to look at the events in terms of regions and thus fail to notice any pattern in the way the mutinies spread across the Gangetic plain. However, the dates of the mutinies do suggest a pattern: 20 May, Aligarh; 23 May, Etawah and Mainpuri; 27 May, Etah;

30 May, Lucknow, and so on down the Gangetic plains. From Lucknow, the mutinies also travelled southwards to Kanpur and Jhansi in Bundelkhand and northwards to Gonda and Bahraich on the Nepalese borders. It does appear from the dates and places that the mutinies were spreading down the Ganges valley from Delhi with just the right time-gap between the various stations required for the news to travel from one place to another.[6]

On 30 May, the mutiny reached Lucknow, the capital of Awadh, a kingdom that had been annexed by Lord Dalhousie in February 1856. That evening, an *emeute* occurred in Lucknow. This was an event waiting to happen. Kaye, who wrote a very early and detailed account of the uprising (he called it the 'Sepoy War') noted that the sepoys in the Lucknow cantonment had been in an 'uncertain state of semi-mutiny' waiting for events to develop 'sufficiently . . . elsewhere to encourage a general rising of the troops at Lucknow.'[7] There had been enough signs that people in Lucknow were tense and anxious since early May when the 7th Regiment of the Awadh Irregular Infantry refused to accept the new cartridges that had been furnished to them.[8] In the days immediately after the fall of Delhi, proclamations in Hindi, Urdu and Persian were put up all over the city calling upon the populace—both Hindus and Muslims—to unite, rise and kill the *firangi*s.[9] People began to display their hatred for the white man by carrying out acts of symbolic violence: figures were dressed up as Europeans and their heads were cut off in public places, much to the amusement and appreciation of the crowd that gathered.[10] Such acts, as studies of popular unrest have shown, frequently occur in, or precede, episodes of insurgency.

To understand this popular anger against the firangi, it is necessary to place the uprising in Lucknow and the rest of Awadh in its historical context. Awadh was one of the earliest successor states of the Mughal Empire; as the latter declined as a centralizing force under a series of incompetent rulers, powerful noblemen began to carve out territories for themselves. In 1722, an important Mughal nobleman, Saadat Khan, refused the imperial order transferring him to Malwa and declared himself the independent ruler of Awadh based in Lucknow.[11] Since then, Awadh had been a sprawling principality flourishing in the heart of north India. The word 'flourishing' is used advisedly. Muzaffar Alam has shown that Awadh was one of the areas where economic growth was noticeable within the overall decline of the Mughal Empire in the eighteenth century.[12] Awadh's first brush with the English East India Company and therefore with British rule was at the battle of Baksar in October 1764, when the then Nawab of Awadh, Shuja-ud-Daula, joined forces with the Mughal Emperor, Shah Alam, and the Nawab of Bengal, Mir Qasim, to form a tripartite alliance against the British. Defeat at Baksar made Shuja-ud-Daula accept the terms set by the British, which included permission to the Company to trade in Awadh, agree to pay a subsidy to the British, ostensibly for the maintenance of a garrison of British troops for his 'protection', and have the presence in his court of a British Resident. Thus began a relationship that was one-sided in favour of the British. Awadh, as one historian has pithily put it, became increasingly important not for what it could do, but for what it had to offer.[13] This relationship and British trade sapped Awadh of its economic resources, and the growth of the trade and its changing nature served as the context for the truncation of the nawab's territory by Lord Wellesley in 1801.[14]

Through the Resident, the British also established control over the administration and reduced the nawab (called a king by the British from 1819) into a figurehead. The situation was summed up by the historian Thomas Metcalf thus:

> With the subsidiary alliance drawn tightly about him, he could not ignore the British and act as before. But he had neither the training nor the military force to act upon the injunction of his European advisers. So the Nawabs who succeeded Saadat Ali Khan (post 1814), one after the other, increasingly abandoned the attempt to govern and retired into the *zanana*, where they amused themselves with wine, women and poetry. The sensuous life . . . did not reflect sheer perversity or weakness of character on the part of the Nawabs. Indolence was rather the only appropriate response to the situation in which the princes of Oudh were placed: in which they could not be overthrown but could not act effectively in either the old way or the new.[15]

Metcalf also notes that this plight of the nawabs was pointed out by some British officers, like F.J. Shore and Henry Lawrence. This enforced inability to rule was interpreted by most British officials, especially Lord Dalhousie, as incompetence and a refusal to rule. Using misgovernment as a pretext, Dalhousie annexed Awadh on 7 February 1856 and sent the king Wajid Ali Shah to exile in Calcutta.

The annexation and the treatment meted out to Wajid Ali Shah caused an emotional upheaval in Lucknow and the countryside of Awadh. Having condemned Wajid Ali Shah as an incompetent ruler, the British had not quite reckoned with the fact that he was a popular king, much loved by his subjects. The annexation was resented: a folk song of the time lamented: *Angrez Bahadur ain: mulk lain linho* (the honourable English came and took the country).[16] When Wajid Ali Shah left Lucknow for the last time to go to Calcutta, many of his subjects followed him all the way to Kanpur singing dirges. A contemporary wrote, 'The condition of this town [Lucknow] without any exaggeration was such that it appeared that on the departure of Jan-i Alam, the life was gone out of the body, and the body of this town had been left lifeless . . . there was no street or market and house which did not wail out the cry of agony in separation of Jan-i Alam.'[17] A folk song of the period echoed the sentiments: 'Noble and peasant all wept together/ and all the world wept and wailed/Alas! The chief has bidden adieu to/ his country and gone abroad.'[18]

The land revenue policies the British adopted in Awadh caused a different kind of upheaval in the countryside. The Summary Settlement of 1856 was directed against the *taluqdars*, who held real power in the rural world as large landholders with forts and retainers. British land revenue policy considered taluqdars as interlopers who stood between the government and the peasants. The British destroyed many of the forts and through the Summary Settlement dispossessed the taluqdars of large parts of their landholding. The Summary Settlement halved the holdings of the taluqdars. Furthermore, in many of the districts the land revenue assessment was pitched higher than it had been in nawabi times.[19] The reverberations of these developments in rural Awadh and the exile of the king were felt keenly in the sepoy lines, as most of the sepoys of the Bengal Army came from southern Awadh. This entire amalgam of interrelated issues was communicated to Captain Barrow by Hanwant Singh, who had provided him protection during the uprising. When the latter was sending Barrow off to Allahabad, Hanwant Singh told him: 'Sahib, your countrymen came into this country and drove out our king. You sent your officers round the districts to examine the titles to the estates. At one blow you took from me lands which from time immemorial had been in my family. I submitted. Suddenly misfortune fell upon you. The people of the land rose against you. You came to me whom you had despoiled. I have saved you. But now—now I march at the head of my retainers to Lakhnao to try and drive you out of the country.'[20]

This context helps to understand what happened in Lucknow after the mutiny erupted. Henry Lawrence had expressed his anxiety about the districts of Awadh.[21] As things unfolded there, there was a replay of what had happened after the fall of Delhi and the transmission of the news. The cantonments in the districts had been waiting for the developments in Lucknow. Once the Lucknow garrison had raised the flag of mutiny, the other cantonments followed in quick succession: Sitapur, Faizabad, Gonda-Bharaich, Sultanpur and Salon. The fall of one station, since it signalled the weakness—and even the fall—of British power, contributed to the rising of another garrison. After they had mutinied, the sepoys, the villagers, the taluqdars and their retainers marched to Lucknow exactly as Hanwant Singh had told Barrow. By the end of June, a large rebel army—

7000 to 8000 strong[22]—was ready to descend on Lucknow, where, under the orders of Henry Lawrence, the entire British population had taken refuge in the Residency. The inevitable military encounter—the first between the British and the rebels—took place on the last day of June at Chinhat. The British were defeated and had to retreat. The news of the loss had an electrifying impact in Lucknow and in other parts of Awadh. It was taken as a fact that British rule had 'past [sic] away forever and the "Nawabee" is restored as a matter of course.'[23] The siege of the Residency commenced, and the victory was celebrated with groups of rebels going round the streets of Lucknow chanting 'Bom Mahadeo'. Away from the streets and the people, steps were taken to bring back and establish the political order that had existed before the annexation. It was not possible to bring back Wajid Ali Shah, so powerful taluqdars and former ministers conferred and decided to put Wajid Ali Shah's twelve-year-old son, Birjis Qadr, on the throne on 5 July.[24] The rebels embraced the new king. 'You are Kanahaiya [Krishna],' they said. It was during the preparations for the coronation that Hazrat Mahal made her entry into the annals of the uprising and thus on the stage of history.

Who was Hazrat Mahal apart from being the mother of the new king and therefore the wife and the Begum of Wajid Ali Shah? This is where historians begin to tread on relatively unknown territory. Little is known about her. The scattered and often unconfirmed bits of evidence have been very carefully stitched together by the historian Rosie Llewellyn-Jones.[25] According to her, Hazrat Mahal came from a very humble background—her father was an African slave. She joined the Pari Khanna music school in Lucknow. Members of this school had Pari (fairy) suffixed to their names; thus, she was called Mahak Pari. Through her talents or good looks or both, she caught the eye and the fancy of Wajid Ali Shah, who made her into one of his many *muta* (temporary wives). In 1845, she gave birth to a son, and this led to her being elevated by Wajid Ali Shah to the position of Mahal (a title that Wajid Ali Shah gave to his better placed wives, according to Sharar)[26] and she came to be styled Nawab Iftikhar un-Nisa Begum Hazrat Mahal Sahiba. In 1850, fortune stopped smiling on Hazrat Mahal. That year Wajid Ali Shah gave talaq to six wives, including Hazrat Mahal, who was dismissed from the harem. It was rumoured at the time that the king's mother, who wielded considerable influence over him, had persuaded him to disassociate himself from his wives who were of lowly origin. The divorce and the dismissal from the zanana meant that when Wajid Ali Shah was forced to leave Lucknow for Calcutta, Hazrat Mahal did not find a place in his entourage. It is also entirely possible that the talaq and the exit from the royal household implied that she had been stripped of her fancy title. She was officially no longer a begum. But through a quirk of fate, her son became the king and the *wali* (governor)[27] of the Mughal Badshah and thus she regained her title of Begum. She became the power behind the throne in Awadh and all orders that emanated in the name of Birjis Qadr were hers. A rebellion of the people had made her a leader, and she became the leader of the people.

*

Jhansi was a small principality in Bundelkhand. The mutiny occurred there on 5 June. Robert Hamilton, a British officer

in 1857, had heard from a sepoy whom he considered
trustworthy that someone belonging to the 12th Native
Infantry had brought a chit from Delhi stating that 'the
whole army of the Bengal Presidency had mutinied and as
the Regiment stationed at Jhansee had not done so—men
composing it were outcasts or had lost their faith.'[28] This
accusation spurred the sepoys to action in Jhansi. Things
moved swiftly. On the afternoon of 5 June, sepoys of the
12th Native Infantry raised an alarm that dacoits had
attacked the magazine. They rushed to the Star Fort and
seized the magazine and Rs 47 lakh. Some British officers
were fired at. Following this, all the British officials and
officers with their families took shelter at the Jhansi fort.
The following day, the entire garrison was up in arms. They
broke open the jail and set fire to bungalows where the
British lived. A group of rebels headed up to the town and
opened the Orcha gate to the cry 'Deen ki jai'. They went
to the palace where the rani lived and demanded assistance
from her. The guards meant to protect her deserted and
joined the rebels, who then laid siege to the fort where
the British had taken refuge. The siege continued for two
days, with some of the British officers killed in gunfire. The
British decided to surrender on the condition that their lives
be spared. The sepoys agreed. But as soon as the British
exited the fort they were bound, taken to Jhokun Bagh and
massacred. Jhansi, like all the other towns of north India,
was free of British rule. The triumphant sepoys sped off to
Delhi on 12 June, carrying with them as much treasure as
they could.[29]

The persona of the Rani of Jhansi has already tip-toed
into the narrative. It is time to introduce her but before we

do that, it is necessary to provide a brief history of Jhansi just prior to the uprising. This will help put in perspective who the rani was and how she was placed in the summer of 1857.

Jhansi, despite its small size, had a chequered history. It was merely a *subahadari,* or governor's province, under the Peshwas in the eighteenth century when the Maratha power was spreading out beyond the Maratha Desh. Chhatrasal Bundela, the king of Bundelkhand, had gifted Peshwa Baji Rao I one third of his territories in 1731 for his help in resisting the advance of Mughal power into Bundelkhand. Through this division, Baji Rao I acquired a portion of Bundelkhand that included Jhansi and yielded a revenue of Rs 33 lakhs.[30] The Peshwa divided his Bundelkhand territories into three provinces and appointed a *subahadar* for each of them. Jhansi was given to Raghunath Hari Nevalkar, in whose family the governorship became hereditary. Nevalkar stepped down in favour of his brother Shivram Bhau, with whom the British entered into an agreement in 1804. In 1817, after Baji Rao II surrendered to the British, this agreement became a treaty between the British government and Ramchandra Rao, the grandson and heir of Shivram Bhau. By this treaty, the British acknowledged that 'Row Ramchund, his heirs and successors, [as] hereditary rulers of the territory enjoyed by the late Row Sheo Bhow . . . excepting Pergunnah Mote.'[31] In 1832, the then Governor General Lord William Bentinck, during his tour of north and central India, visited Jhansi, where he was received with a show of grandeur and pomp.[32] Following this visit, Ramchandra Rao was invested with the title Maharajadhiraj Fidvi Badshah Jamjah Inglistan (Devoted Servant of the Glorious King of England). A former subahadar of the Marathas was thus declared a king subordinate to the British monarch. Jhansi became a kingdom under a new king.

A few years later, Ramchandra Rao died childless in 1835. His widow adopted her sister's son, but this succession was disputed. The British government intervened and proffered the title and the kingdom to Raghunath Rao, Shivram Bhau's son and Ramchandra Rao's uncle. Raghunath Rao turned out to be an incompetent and debauched ruler, and under him the kingdom of Jhansi sank into bankruptcy and ruin. Once again, the British government came to govern the kingdom. Jhansi was in fact ruled by the British even before it was officially annexed. Raghunath Rao died without an heir and a dispute over the succession ensued. The British decided to settle the question by recognizing Gangadhar Rao, the surviving brother of the last Maharaja, as king. But Gangadhar Rao was not allowed to rule Jhansi until 1843. He died in November 1853 without a biological heir, but the day before his death he adopted a boy from another branch of the family. This adoption took place in the presence of the nobles of his court, the political agent of Jhansi, Major Ellis, and the officer commanding the Jhansi contingents, Captain Martin. The king handed over to Major Ellis a silk bag containing a *kharita* (letter) requesting the British government to look after his widow and his son: 'The administration of the state should be vested in my widow during her lifetime as the sovereign of this principality and mother of the child adopted.'[33] In a memorandum that the widowed rani subsequently sent to the Governor General, she pointed out that in Datia and Orcha, as well as in Bundela territories like Jhansi, the claims of an adopted son had been recognized. Major Ellis supported this position and plea. But

Major Malcolm, the Governor General's agent, did not share Ellis's views. When the matter reached Lord Dalhousie, the then Governor General, he argued that the case of Jhansi and of those of Datia and Orcha were not comparable since Jhansi had never been an independent sovereign state. It had been a subahadari under the Peshwas and had subsequently become totally subordinate to the British. In March 1854, under Dalhousie's Doctrine of Lapse policy, Jhansi became a part of the growing British Empire in India. Justifying his decision, Dalhousie noted, 'As it (Jhansi) lies in the midst of other British districts, the possession of it as our own will tend to the improvement of the general internal administration of our possessions in Bundelkhand. That its incorporation with the British territories will be greatly for the benefit of the people of Jhansi a reference to the results of experience will suffice to show.'[34]

It is said that when Ellis communicated the decision regarding the annexation of Jhansi to the rani, she cried out in a defiant and spirited way, '*Meri Jhansi nahi dungi!*'[35] There was some irony in that declaration: Jhansi had never been hers to begin with. She had married into the family that ruled Jhansi first on behalf of the Peshwas and later through the sanction of the British based on the acceptance of British paramountcy. At best, it was a statement of her sense of belonging: she belonged to Jhansi; Jhansi did not belong to her.

Named Manikarnika at birth, she came to be called Lakshmibai after her marriage to Gangadhar Rao. Her father was Moropant Tambe and her mother Bhagirathi Bai. The historian Tapti Roy writes that the Tambes were Karhade Brahmins from Vai in Satara.[36] Moropant was in the retinue of Chimnaji Appa, the brother of Baji Rao II, who had settled in Varanasi after the Peshwas surrendered to the British in 1818. The exact date of Manikarnika's birth is a matter of speculation in the absence of hard evidence. A Marathi book by D.B. Parasnis, published in 1894, on the Rani of Jhansi says, without citing any evidence, that she was born on 19 November 1835.[37] Roy notes that there is one date about which there is no doubt: Chimnaji Appa died in June 1832. His death meant that Moropant Tambe had lost his patron. He was forced to look for alternative sources of livelihood. The former Peshwa Baji Rao II offered him employment; this meant that Moropant and his family had to move to Bithur, where Baji Rao II was based. When this move happened, his daughter was three years old. If his daughter was indeed born in 1835, it would mean that Moropant stayed on in Varanasi until 1838, six years after the death of Chimnaji Appa. This seems highly unlikely. It seems logical to assume, given the importance of earning a livelihood, that he moved to Bithur a very short time after his patron's death. This would suggest that his daughter, who was three when he moved to Bithur, was born any time between 1829 and 1830.[38] Whichever date we take—late-1820s or mid-1830s—it is clear that when she was widowed, Lakshmibai was in her twenties.

The name Manikarnika suggests, according to S.N. Sen, that she was born in Varanasi;[39] it is equally important to remember that like her mother, she, too, was named after the river Ganga. While it does not necessarily follow that she was born in Varanasi, it could indeed be a possibility, given that her father lived and worked there at least till 1832. Sen further comments, 'About her childhood we know next to nothing.'[40] While this may be factually correct, her later career throws some light on what she may have learnt or acquired as a growing girl. It is well-established, for example, that she was a fine equestrian and skilled in arms and warfare. She could not have learnt horse riding, archery, or how to wield a *tulwar* and use a gun overnight. These skills demand training and practice. It is not unreasonable to assume that she must have been introduced to them early on in her life. Her upbringing could not have been conventional since very few, if any, Maratha girls were instructed in such skills. This made a biographer writing in the 1960s describe the young Manikarnika as a 'tomboy of great force'.[41] This could be a bit of an overstatement that exhibits some of the prejudices of the author. Manikarnika learnt certain things which were—and probably still are—considered male skills, but this should not undermine the fact that she was a pious woman carrying out all the rituals expected of a Brahmin girl of her time and that she was also a devout wife. It is enough to describe her as an unusual and talented woman without adding any other loaded epithet.

Manikarnika's marriage to Gangadhar Rao was arranged, as was customary, through a matchmaker-cum-astrologer. After her marriage she was given the name Lakshmibai, and that is how she entered the pages of history. Roy dates the wedding to May 1842 and provides a description of it,[42] but neither the date nor the description is based on documentary evidence. If the date is valid, Manikarnika was either seven years old or fourteen or fifteen, depending on when she was born. It was Gangadhar Rao's second marriage, and according to Sen, he was considerably older than his new bride.[43] According to Roy, in November 1851 Lakshmibai gave birth to a son who lived for only three months.[44] The writer provides no evidence for this claim.

Historical documentation is available regarding how Lakshmibai chose to handle the fact of annexation once the decision to annex Jhansi was conveyed to her by Ellis. The terms of the takeover guaranteed the widowed rani a life pension of Rs 60,000 and a residency in the city palace; the fort would be taken over by the British. She would be exempted from the jurisdiction of British courts. The annexation, however, did not overturn the adoption: the adopted son, Damodar Rao, then five years of age, would be heir to the family treasures and Gangadhar Rao's personal property.[45] Lakshmibai was reluctant to accept the annexation as a fait accompli. After one of his visits to her, Ellis reported to his superiors that 'she seems to entertain an idea that the orders of government in her case are not considered as final.'[46] She sent her lawyer to Gwalior to meet Malcolm, the political agent for Gwalior; Malcolm sent the lawyer to see Hamilton, the agent for Central India, who in no uncertain terms informed the lawyer that the decision on Jhansi was final and would not be changed. Lakshmibai also wrote directly to Dalhousie pleading for time, saying that she had appointed a representative to meet the Governor General and till such time to withhold the imposition of British administration on Jhansi. She asked for a month to convince Dalhousie of the reasons why she was justified in her demand that Jhansi remain independent. If after that, she said, the British were to decide to absorb Jhansi nevertheless, then, 'the 5000 rusty swords worn by the people called its army and its fifty pieces of harmless ordnance will be delivered over to your lordship.'[47] Ellis was sympathetic to Lakshmibai's cause at the risk of his own career. He suggested that she choose John Lang, a barrister-at-law and a journalist, as her representative. Lang visited Jhansi at Lakshmibai's invitation and had a long meeting with her. He was probably the first firangi to actually see Lakshmibai in person. Lang told her that the Governor General was powerless in the matter and the decision could only be reversed in London. Nonetheless, Lang did forward Lakshmibai's letter to Dalhousie, who refused to entertain him. But Lang arrived in Calcutta with Lakshmibai's lawyer. Even though they could not meet any official, the letter yielded a reply: the 'orders for the resumption of Jhansi will not be revoked by the government of India.'

Lakshmibai's final appeal, made in December 1854, was to the court of directors of the English East India Company. Here she pursued a different tack. She made two incontrovertible points. One, she spoke about the 'uninterrupted friendship' between the British government and the rulers of Jhansi. And two, the ceremony of adoption had been carried out in public, not in secret. She made an additional point which was very important. She asked what right the East India Company had to seize Jhansi just because it did not accept adoption. How could the Company do away with, under some pretext or another, the existence of Indian states? She was raising the question of sovereignty and casting doubt on the Company's usurpation of sovereignty. The question bothered many Indian rulers who had been deposed by the Company from the time of Mir Qasim in Bengal in 1763, but Lakshmibai was probably the first to pose it directly to the concerned authorities. She did not receive a reply or an acknowledgement from the court of directors.

By this time, the rani seemed to be reconciled to her fate, because when Hamilton met her in Jhansi in April 1855, she, from behind the purdah, did not complain about the annexation. In fact, she declared herself to be 'wholly dependent' on the British and expressed her gratitude for being excluded from the jurisdiction of the district courts. Her only appeal to Hamilton was that she be placed directly under him, the agent Governor General, and not under the district officials who reported to the Lieutenant-Governor. Although Hamilton forwarded her request to the Governor General, he failed to get the rani's plea passed. The failure may have been related to the fact that A. Skene, who had replaced Ellis, reported that in the course of a meeting with her, Lakshmibai had requested that she be placed under more senior officers. When Skene explained to her lawyer that such a change would not alter matters and that he was treating her with utmost respect, Lakshmibai seemed satisfied. Skene said that from behind the purdah, she was 'so far satisfied with the position assigned to her by government, that she had no wish to change it, feeling that her rank (would) be respected and her interests cared for in every way.' Roy very rightly asks: Was the rani really satisfied, or was this Skene's impression? The problem of misrepresentation and misinterpretation in a conversation carried out through an interpreter was a real one in the middle of the nineteenth century.[48]

Kaye's summing up of Lakshmibai's attempts to negotiate with the British bears quotation. He wrote: 'So Jhansi was resumed. In vain the widow of the late Rajah . . . protested that her husband's House had ever been faithful to the British Government—in vain she dwelt upon services rendered in former days to that government, and the acknowledgements which they had elicited from our rulers—in vain she pointed to the terms of the treaty, which did not, to her simple understanding, bar succession in accordance with the laws and usages of her country—in vain she quoted precedents to show that the grace and favour sought for Jhansi had been yielded to other states. The fiat was irrevocable.'[49]

Even after Lakshmibai had reconciled herself to the reality of the annexation, she discovered that there was more humiliation in store for her and Jhansi. One of the first policy measures of the British added salt to her wounds. The British resumed the villages that had been assigned to the temple of Mahalakshmi, the family deity of the ruling family, and tried to placate the rani by adding Rs 1000 to her pension. After Lakshmibai had overcome her initial reluctance to accept the pension in the first place, she discovered that she was expected to pay off her late husband's debts from it. These were not Gangadhar Rao's personal debts, she argued, but of the state of Jhansi. The matter was not resolved. Upon annexation, she discovered that there was a cash balance of Rs 6 lakh in the treasury; the British government had held this money in trust for the minor son of the king. The rani asked the government for Rs 1 lakh from this fund to meet the expenses of her son's sacred thread ceremony. The British government refused to disburse this amount unless the rani provided four guarantors for its repayment in case the boy demanded the entire amount after coming of age. The rani justifiably resented this demand for sureties. Her grievances merged with the dismay of the people when the British government permitted cow slaughter, something that had always been prohibited in Jhansi.[50]

The military and administrative dominance that the British imposed on the region, the treatment meted out to the widowed rani and the dismantling of existing practices compounded the impact of the sudden and unfair annexation. This was because, according to Malcolm, Lakshmibai was 'much respected by everyone in Jhansi.'[51] In her conversations with British officials, Lakshmibai had more than once spoken of her desire to move to Varanasi to live in retirement. This worried the British: Hamilton noted that this would not only upset the people of Jhansi but also 'entail serious loss on the town, in which she was the occasion of a good deal of money being circulated.'[52] The nature of British rule was in sharp contrast to the way Gangadhar Rao had ruled Jhansi. He appears to have been a typical paternalistic ruler: a kind man who was a patron of arts and letters, especially of theatre.[53] Dalhousie, as he was to do in the case of Awadh in 1856, had deliberately ignored the emotional turmoil the annexation would wreak. These sentiments chimed with the complaints of the sepoys when the latter mutinied in early June. In Jhansi, like in every other station in north India, it ceased to be a mere mutiny since the common people joined hands with the sepoys to transform it into a general uprising.

The events of early June 1857 placed the rani in an unenviable position. Many people in Jhansi—her former subjects—had rebelled against British rule and killed many British men, women and children. She could not have been unaware of these events even though she had not emerged from her palace. She could not, her own grievances notwithstanding, overlook the long history of friendship that had existed between the British government and the ruling house of Jhansi. As soon as the rebels sped off towards Delhi, she wrote two letters to commissioner and agent W.C. Erskine, also Lieutenant-Governor, Sagar division. These letters were carried by *harkaras* concealed in walking sticks. In a letter (possibly dated 12 June) Lakshmibai wrote:

> The Govt. Forces, stationed at Jhansi, thro' their faithlessness, cruelty and violence, killed all the European Civil and Military Officers, the clerks and all their families and the Ranee not being able to assist them for want of guns and soldiers . . . she could render them no aid which she very much regrets. That they the mutineers afterwards behaved with much violence against herself and servants, and extorted a great deal of money from her, and said that as the Ranee was entitled to succeed to the Reasut (*riyasat*) she should undertake the management since the Sepoys were proceeding to Delhi to the King . . . her dependence was entirely on the British authorities who met with such a misfortune the Sepoys knowing her to be quite helpless sent her messages to the effect that if she, at all hesitated to comply with their requests, they would blow up her palace with guns. Taking into consideration her position she was obliged to consent to all the requests made . . . and had to pay large sums in property, as well as in cash to save her life and honour. Knowing that no British Officers had been spared in the whole District, she was in consideration of the welfare and protection of the people, and the District, induced to address Perwannahs to all the Govt subordinate Agency in the shape of Police &c to remain at their posts and perform their duties as usual, she is in continual dread of her own life and that of the inhabitants.[54]

This document has been read, not incorrectly, as a statement on the rani's part to exonerate herself from what had happened in Jhansi and to make an open declaration of her own helplessness. Sen commented, 'there [was] nothing clandestine in this straightforward communication.'[55] There are two other points that need to be highlighted. One is that the sepoys, before they left for Delhi, made it clear that she was entitled to the riyasat and the management of Jhansi was her responsibility. The other is that she herself had assumed this responsibility for 'the welfare and protection of the people and the district.' In other words, she had undertaken the queen's duties at the behest of the sepoys. It is significant that on the evening the British had been massacred in Jhansi the sepoys had issued a proclamation which said: 'The people are God's, the country is the Padshah's and the two religions govern.'[56] Immediately after the sepoys left for Delhi, Lakshmibai issued a second proclamation: 'Raj is Lachmee Bai's.'[57] She put up her flag on the fort, established a mint and demanded *nazrana* from the *mahajan*s. She had indeed declared herself a rani.

This is how two women—one in Lucknow and the other in Jhansi—both from relatively obscure and humble backgrounds, through the accident of marriage, found themselves in the summer of 1857 in the embrace of an uprising of the people.

REBELLION

The mutiny in Lucknow was different from the mutinies in the other stations of north India, in that the emeute in Lucknow was not followed by wholesale slaughter of the firangi. Killing did happen but not on the scale of what took place in Jhansi or Meerut.[1] The principal reason was the decision taken by Henry Lawrence to steer the white population of Lucknow to the safety of the Residency before 30 May, the evening the sepoys rose in revolt. Once the rebel army had defeated the British forces at Chinhat, the insurgents concentrated all their efforts at bombarding the Residency and throwing the British out of Lucknow. The Residency was surrounded, one report said, with as many as 35,000 rebels (sepoys and retainers of the taluqdars); the report added: 'Everyday their numbers increase.'[2] The situation for those within the Residency was so dire that Lawrence thought they could hold out for a maximum of 15 to 20 days.[3]

The report just quoted also said, 'Orders have been sent to all the Talooqdars to repair with all their retainers to Lucknow.' The rebels, the report continued, 'are repairing all the guns of the late Native Government which the English disabled at annexation.' A workshop was set up in Faizabad to repair heavy guns. Supply lines of ammunition from the districts were maintained. A huge quantity of lead was discovered and then converted into bullets.[4] Percussion caps and all kinds of ammunition were being produced in Lucknow and artisans had been especially brought in from Delhi.[5] These scraps— and they are no more than scraps—suggest that there was a concerted attempt made to defeat the British. Such an attempt could not have been possible without a decision-making body that was overseeing and guiding operations. That body existed in the court of Hazrat Mahal. It was from this court that orders emanated and plans of attack and resistance were formulated. One witness testified, 'When the Court assembled at the Begum's door . . . all the members of the Govt. used to attend as well as the Comdts.'[6] One report gives the names of those who attended this court: Jailal Singh, Mummoo Khan, Shur-od-Dowla, Hissam-od-Dowla (15th Irregular Cavalry), Mukdoom Bux, Gummendee Singh, Ousan Singh, Omorow Singh, Bahadur Ally, Rughonat Singh, Misri Singh, Gujadhur Singh, Raj Mund Teewaree, Bakht Khan, Wajid Ally Khan, Shahbadee Khan, Meer Wazeer Ally (912th Irre. Cavalry), Sheikh Sukhun, Ressaldar, Moulvee Mostan, Ressaldar and others. They met in the Tara Kothee two or three times a week and the deliberations were submitted to Hazrat Mahal.[7] This court, in the name of Birjis Qadr, issued ishtahars urging people to fight to save their religions; the proclamations also condemned the British rule in the strongest possible terms.

The court appointed two different bodies: one to look after administration, payments etc., and a second one to manage and direct the military affairs. The former consisted of ex-bureaucrats of the nawabi administration:

Sharafuddaulah, naib (minister or deputy); Mummoo Khan, *daroga* (superintendent of a department) of the Diwan Khana (Hall of Audience); Mir Wajid Ali, Naib of the Diwan Khana; Mir Kasim Ali, daroga of the magazine; Maharaja Bal Kishen, Diwan; Munshi Thakur Dayal, household munshi and paymaster; Mir Mehendi, chief of the intelligence department; Ahmed Hussein, daroga of Nazul (government land); Sewak Ram, naib of Thakur Dayal; Munshi Amir Hyder, Sahib-e-Duskut (in charge of royal letters); Muzaffar Ali Khan, General; Raja Jai Lal Singh, collector.[8]

The military cell consisted mostly of sepoys or rebel soldiers, as well as some of the above officials: Sheikh Sukun Rissaladar Weston's Horse; Wajid Ali Khan Rissaladar (commander) 1st Oudh Irregular Cavalry; Jehangir Khan, Artillery; Ghamandi Singh of Captain Orr's Regiment; Raghunath Singh, captain of police battalion; Burkat Ahmed Rissaladar of the 12th Irregular Cavalry; Mummoo Khan; Muzuffur Ali Khan; Sangum Singh Captain Begum's New Regiment; Surju Singh; Raja Jai Lal Singh. The latter liaised between the two bodies and the begum.[9]

This court also sent out *hukumnama*s (orders), in the name of Birjis Qadr, to various taluqdars.[10] The nature of the resistance that the British encountered is testimony to the fact that these urgings were not in vain. Describing the situation around the Residency, one officer wrote, 'They soon had twenty to twenty-five guns in position, some of them of very large calibre, which were planted all round our post at small distances, some being actually within fifty yards of our defences, but in places where our own heavy guns could not reply to them; while the perseverance and ingenuity of the enemy in erecting barricades in front of, and around their guns in a very short time, rendered all attempts to silence them by musketry entirely unavailing. Neither could they be effectively silenced by shells, by reason of their extreme proximity to our position, and because moreover, the enemy had recourse to digging very narrow trenches, about eight feet in depth, in rear of each gun; in which the men lay while our shells were flying, and which so effectually concealed them, even while working the gun, that our baffled sharpshooters could only see their hands while in the act of loading.'[11]

Beyond the walls of the Residency, out in the villages, ordinary villagers put up a resistance against a column headed by Henry Havelock and James Outram and moving from Kanpur to Lucknow to offer relief to those who were besieged in the Residency. One officer wrote, 'Every village is held against us, the zemindars have risen to oppose us . . . We know them to be all around us in bodies of 500 or 600 independent of the regular levies.'[12] These pockets of resistance often contained acts of heroism like this: 'The pertinacity of one of the villagers . . . was remarkable. He had stationed himself in a little mud fort at the entrance of the place [Bashihatganj in Unao] . . . and had contrived to hide himself, thus escaping the fate of his comrades in the general bayoneting. As soon as the main body of the English had passed on, this man emerged from his shelter, and plied his solitary matchlock with effect at the guns, the baggage, the elephants . . . the poor wretch was shot through the head as he was crossing over the parapet for a last hit at his enemies.'[13]

Apart from the fighting, there was jubilation and celebration on the streets of Lucknow. People distributed halwa, puri and sweets, while also indulging in 'spicy and tasteful food'. The wealthy were taunted and plundered.[14]

Noting such exhibitions of popular revelry, a historian has gone to the extent of calling them a 'festival of the oppressed'.[15] There certainly was a sense of liberation at the passing of British rule. But signs of fracture were also appearing. Those who hailed Birjis Qadr as Kanhaiya warned him, 'Be cautious of turbaned men.'[16] It was an obvious reference to the rich and the privileged. The Court was already receiving complaints about the misdeeds of those who saw themselves to be powerful in the new government. One letter writer noted, '. . . the chiefs of the army draw the salaries of the sipahis and the sawars [horsemen] but do not distribute them, rather keep the money with themselves without giving a single shell from it to the sipahis. If any the wise army officers were to carry on the administration of the army, no case of disobedience would take place . . .'[17] It fell upon Hazrat Mahal to hold the rebellion together.

The rebels' efforts suffered a setback when the approaching column successfully broke through the rebel lines and entered the Residency on 25 September 1857. This event came to be labelled by the British around the end of the nineteenth century as the 'First Relief of Lucknow.' In reality, it was no 'relief' at all. Having entered the Residency, Havelock and Outram discovered to their dismay that they were trapped, and the British in the Residency were still under siege. They were isolated, with their supply lines cut off, and surrounded by rebels. Outram wrote to his commander–in–chief on 31 September, 'To force our way through the city would have proved a very desperate operation, if indeed it could have been accomplished.'[18] A few days later he sent a telegram saying that 'the insurgents are too strong to admit of withdrawing.'[19] The rebels too realized this, and their morale remained high. The leadership rejected every overture made by Outram to arrive at a negotiated settlement.[20]

Lucknow became the focus of both the resistance and the British counter-insurgency measures. Both sides realized the importance of controlling the city. A few days before he entered the Residency to provide what he thought was relief, Outram had cabled Canning: 'The moral effect of abandoning Lucknow will be very serious against us; the many well-disposed chiefs in Oude and Rohilcund, who are now watching the turn of affairs, would regard the loss of Lucknow as the forerunner of the end of our rule.'[21] Two months after his entry, he reiterated the point, 'I regard the re-establishment of our Government as an impossibility, so long as the capital, which is looked upon by every native as the seat of government, is in the hands of the rebels.'[22] Khan Bahadur Khan, the rebellion leader in Barreilly and Rohilkhand with very close links with Hazrat Mahal's court and the revolt in Awadh, noted: '. . . There are still two places, Barreilly and Lucknow (which is an imperial city) against which the efforts of the British have been unsuccessful . . . If God be with us, it (British rule) shall never be again known in these two cities. If the English are kept in check at Barreilly and if Lucknow is not threatened, assistance will certainly reach Barreilly from the last mentioned city of Lucknow is taken by the English Barreilly must fall but if on the contrary Barreilly is first taken by the British it can easily be reconquered by the assistance of the Oudh troops.'[23] The rebels concentrated a large number of forces in Lucknow—responding to the appeals and orders from the court 'almost all the Talookdars sent men and agents' to Lucknow.[24]

Developments outside Awadh were also exerting their influence on what was happening in Lucknow. By the end of September and early October, the uprising in Delhi had been suppressed and the old Mughal capital had been reconquered, with British authority re-established. The rebels who had been defeated in Delhi now turned their attention to Lucknow, which was still resisting the British forces, remaining outside their control. Lucknow was the place where the cause could still be defended and fought for; it was also a haven with access to money, food and shelter. Through October and November, rebels flocked to Lucknow to increase their numbers.[25] Hazrat Mahal called upon these new arrivals in the name of *khuda* to help her. This appeal was urgent and they joined the battle immediately.[26] Some important taluqdars like Lal Madho Singh of Amethi had warned Hazrat Mahal that the British forces under Colin Campbell were advancing towards Lucknow and needed to be stopped before they reached Alambagh.[27] When Campbell and his army finally entered Lucknow to relieve the people entrapped in the Residency, there were more than 50,000 fighting men there.[28]

Colin Campbell evacuated the British from the city in November 1857. This had the opposite effect to what he had intended: 'It was then proclaimed in the city that the Europeans had abandoned the place and addresses to the same purport were sent to the district authorities and to the king of Delhie. The Chief Begum has given Shurruffooddowlah written instructions to occupy Benares and Allahabad, and the Nuwab is making the necessary military preparations to carry out these orders. Councils of war are constantly being held . . . The War is now fully believed throughout Lucknow to be a religious crusade, and crowds of people are flocking into the capital from the districts to take part in the struggle.'[29] In January 1858, it was estimated that the rebel army in Lucknow was more than 100,000 strong.[30] The feeling was that even though the British forces had left for now, they would soon be back. Efforts were thus concentrated to make such a return impossible or as difficult as possible by reinforcing Lucknow. About 15,000 workmen were employed to build fortifications; a deep moat was dug around the Kaiserbagh to let in water from the Gomti. In addition, 'every street and lane [was] barricaded . . . and all the houses loopholed.'[31] It is important to underline that such projects of extensive fortification would not have been possible in the absence of central direction and planning, nor without an allocation of resources. This is where the Court of Hazrat Mahal played a crucial role. This is important to bear in mind because the uprising has often been portrayed by many British historians since the late nineteenth century as mindless violence by the soldiery. The rebellion had a mind or many minds. All the decisions may not have emanated directly from Hazrat Mahal, but they certainly came from a court of which she was not only an integral part, but also likely the one who asked for it to be set up.

The leadership and authority of Hazrat Mahal and her court did not go unopposed in Lucknow. The main challenge came from Maulavi Ahmadullah Shah, about whose antecedents not much is known. According to one testimony, the maulavi declared himself a disciple of Mehrab Shah, a holy man who lived and preached in Gwalior.[32] He said he had lived in Gwalior for a long time before moving to Agra, where he preached as a fakir. He also moved around in other parts of the North-Western Provinces propagating a holy war against the British. In 1857, during the uprising, he was around forty. According to this informant, the maulavi was a man of little learning, with a smattering of Persian, Arabic and even English. He claimed to have visited England and spoke with 'great apparent familiarity' regarding places in England. After the annexation of Awadh, he arrived in Faizabad, where he continued to preach and gather men to avenge the death of Maulavi Amir Ali, who had died fighting at Hanumangarhi just before the annexation. For this he was arrested by the British, but when the sepoys in Faizabad broke open the jail, he was freed. He moved to Lucknow and was present at the battle of Chinhat.[33] At Chinhat he 'fought stubbornly' and was wounded in the foot.[34]

During the battle against the British in Lucknow, the maulavi proclaimed he was invincible and 'impressed his followers with the belief that his whip and handkerchief possessed magical qualities'. He prophesied complete success and thus won the support of many people.[35] The initial success of the rebels in Lucknow won the maulavi many supporters, first among the Muslims and then among non-Muslims too. He was seen as a prophet. On the basis of this support and his claim of having the sanction of divine will, the maulavi threatened to set himself up as king and demanded that Hazrat Mahal and Birjis Qadr become his disciples.[36] He thus became an alternative centre of power. The sepoys and rebels from Delhi and other places rallied under the banner of the maulavi. But the Awadh regiments and the Najeebs stood by Hazrat Mahal and her son.[37]

The inevitable clash between the maulavi and his supporters and Hazrat Mahal and her loyalists occurred around mid-January 1858. A British intelligence report said, 'The exact cause is not clearly known. Some say that the Maulvee commenced to form a bridge of boats across the river near his residence at Ghaoghat and that Mummoo Khan sent a force to compel him to desist . . . Others again state that the Maulvee issued a "hidayah Namah" to the boy King whose mother then desired the soldiers to declare either for him or for the Maulvee and on their declaring for him (Birjis Qadr) she ordered them to seize the Maulvee . . . this is certain that a fight did take place and that a large number of men, probably not less than 200, were killed and wounded.'[38]

It is entirely possible that there may have been another encounter on an earlier occasion. Another report said that immediately after the battle of Chinhat, the maulavi's popularity among the rebels ran so high that 'the Begum . . . began to dread his paramount influence as dangerous to her authority.' She therefore organized a force to reduce his power and the 'measures she took did not stop short of open attack.' The maulavi was forced to flee from Lucknow and take up residence in a garden house in the suburbs.[39] The begum's ire was perhaps caused by the fact that immediately after Chinhat, the maulavi had begun to issue proclamations and had 'adopted all the airs and ceremonials of the royalty.'[40]

There was probably a period of truce between these two encounters when both parties fought together to drive away the British troops. This defence, in spite of the conflux of fighting men in Lucknow, proved to be inadequate. It was becoming clear, even to the rebel leadership, that the tide of events was turning in favour of the British. The rebels had failed to take the Residency and repel the relief forces first under Outram and Havelock and then under Colin Campbell.

After Campbell's evacuation of Lucknow, the rebels also failed to defeat the small detachment of 4000 men under Outram, whom Campbell had left behind at Alambagh. From beyond the borders of Awadh, and across north India, came the news of one British victory after another: Delhi had been won by October; by December, Kanpur had been recovered and operations in the Doab had begun. One consequence of these British victories was that the defeated rebel forces flocked to Awadh, especially Lucknow, which was still outside British control and where the banner of rebellion was still held high. The other implication was grim. The British victories meant that the net was closing in on Awadh and Lucknow. The rebel leadership realized this, and they also recognized the failures of their past resistance. In a meeting of the court, Hazrat Mahal summed up the situation thus:

> Great things were promised from the all-powerful Delhie, and my heart used to be gladdened by the communication I used to receive from that city but now the King has been dispossessed and his army scattered, the English have bought over the Seikhs and Rajahs, and have established their Government West, East and South, and communications are cut off; the Nana has been vanquished; and Lucknow is endangered; what is to be done? The whole army is in Lucknow, but it is without courage. Why does it not attack Alumbagh? Is it waiting for the English to be reinforced, and Lucknow to be surrounded? How much longer am I to pay the sepoys for doing nothing? Answer now, and if fight you won't, I shall negotiate with the English to spare my life.[41]

This statement of Hazrat Mahal has a number of points worth highlighting. First was her realistic assessment of the situation, which was obviously based on intelligence that was being brought to her and the court. This fact itself suggests a degree of coordination. Second, it is clear that Hazrat Mahal was the leader and from that position she spoke to the members of the court. Third, the sepoys were being regularly paid. This implies that there existed a system of revenue collection. Hazrat Mahal seemed to lament that this payment had been a waste since they had not been able to deliver the expected results. And finally, there was a mention of a personal reconciliation with the British. If Hazrat Mahal's intention was to boost morale, her speech had the desired effect, for the members of the court assured her in the following terms: 'Fear not, we shall fight, for if we do not we shall be hanged one by one; we have this fear before our eyes.'[42] The determination to go forth into battle was still there but now it was derived from desperation and not from the hope of throwing out the firangi. Hazrat Mahal's speech or appeal, for the historian, opens up two intersecting possibilities. One was the reality of a desperate resistance against a powerful British army; and the other was yielding to, and seeking accommodation from, a superior military power. Hazrat Mahal chose the former path: to fight and not to yield.

Hazrat Mahal's fears became reality as Campbell began to move towards Lucknow at the end of February 1858. Within one month—towards the end of March—the city, the British claimed, was free of rebels. But Campbell's troops met with fierce resistance. The rebels maintained a constant bombardment through day and night. The palaces had to be breached before they could be taken. Fighting was most intense in the narrow lanes, with intermittent firing from the houses, which, as noted earlier, had been loopholed. As was to be expected, the strongest resistance was at the palace of Hazrat Mahal, which could be taken by the British by overcoming 'an obstinate resistance by Pandy'.[43] The scale of the resistance is evident from the following data: 3000 rebels were dead and eighty rebel guns captured.[44] The rest of the army dispersed into the Awadh countryside as the British failed to cut off their escape.[45] Hazrat Mahal herself was in a fort across the Gogra. The taluqdars, alongwith their retainers, went back to their forts and the sepoys began to regroup. The fall of Lucknow did not mean the subjugation of the rest of Awadh.[46] The British had annexed Awadh in 1856 without a shot being fired; in 1858 they had to conquer it through a show of arms. The scale of the challenge that faced the British around late March, early April was clearly spelt out by William Howard Russell, the correspondent of *The Times* who had travelled with the troops to Lucknow. Russell wrote, 'At present all Oudh may be regarded as an enemy's country, for there are very few chiefs who do not still hold out and defy . . . The capture of Lucknow has dispersed the rebels all over the country and reinforced the hands which the rajahs and zemindars have collected around their forts . . . All our machinery of government is broken and destroyed. Our revenue is collected by rebels. Our police has disappeared utterly.'[47]

Before the rebels completely disbanded from Lucknow into the countryside, the rift between the maulavi and Hazrat Mahal surfaced again. The former interfered with the orders from Hazrat Mahal to despatch twelve regiments to stop the advance of Gurkha troops from Gorakhpur.

The regiments started out but halted on receiving a message from the maulavi that pointed out 'that the object of the begum, Shurf-ood Dowlah and others . . . in sending them out was to get rid of them in order that they might give up the city to the British whose rule they were anxious to see re-established. He added that nothing would go well until they made up their minds to slay Shurf-ood Dowlah.'[48] The maulavi achieved the last objective—the killing of Shurfuddaulah—in March 1858, during Campbell's entry into Lucknow, by declaring Shurfuddaulah a traitor.[49] But what is worth highlighting is that this factional fighting notwithstanding, Outram considered the British position in Awadh to be precarious. He made the point that 'even if dissatisfaction became universal and ended in an absolute rupture between the Queen [sic] Mother and the Moulvee our situation would not be materially benefited thereby.'[50]

Russell's point about revenue being collected is worth underlining. It shows that in spite of reversals and defeats, some of the systems of governance that Hazrat Mahal and her court had set up continued to function. The practice of sending out orders to taluqdars for collecting fighting men persisted. Rana Beni Madho, the taluqdar of Sankarpur and the focus of resistance in south-eastern Awadh, received orders from Birjis Qadr (i.e., Hazrat Mahal) to put together '. . . an army of Gohars, royal servants, Taluqdars and others in Baiswara and for keeping them ready.' Beni Madho added, 'In accordance with his royal order I have collected an army of about 10,000 foot soldiers and horsemen of the troops of the Government and of the Taluqdars in Baiswara.'[51] Around this time, Hazrat Mahal in Bahraich district had with her a force of 5000 men and five guns. Other leaders, mostly taluqdars but also the maulavi, were with their own squads—ranging from 1500 to 10,000 men and guns—all strung out around Lucknow.[52] The British authorities noted, 'Our position at the end of this week [early June 1858] is strictly thus: We hold the Lucknow district and the line of road to Cawnpore. Most of our other posts have been abandoned. Towards the north we have a small but efficient force stationed at Chinhut . . . Throughout the country of Oudh the rebels are complete masters and harass all the followers of the British.'[53]

This rebel force was not only prepared to fight the British, but it was also moving against taluqdars who were declaring their loyalty to the British, taking advantage of the situation in which the British troops were slowly but surely advancing into the Awadh countryside. The rebels had orders from Hazrat Mahal to do this. She confiscated Man Singh's estate by a proclamation and settled it with other claimants. In a letter to the British, Man Singh lamented his plight:

I received orders from Major General Outram to put the Goorkhas across the river and I accordingly expelled the rebels from Oudh and Fyzabad and gathered 200 boats at the Ghat and prepared supplies all through my ilaqa . . . I kept up the Oudh ferry, in order that the Bilwa rebels might not be able to reach Bustee . . . It happened that these Bilwa rebels wrote to the Begum complaining . . . They procured (from her) orders to all zemindars, Talooqdars and mutineers to join them and made preparations for my ruin so far that about a week ago all the Talooqdars from Gonda-Bahraich, Buttanpore [sic] collected to the number of 30,000 and 40,000 men . . . The rebels first invested my thana Bindowlee . . . in consequence of my being known as the well-wisher of the British Government all the Talookdars have become my enemies and wish my destruction . . . Now I do not know what to do . . . there being enemies on two sides of me. The receipt of the Begum's order . . . has changed the minds of all both high and low and everyone is elated with pride.[54]

Even in retreat, Hazrat Mahal's orders were acted upon and she was seen as the one to be obeyed. Man Singh was besieged in his fort in Shahganj and the price demanded to be free from further action was 'the gift of 3 lakhs of Rupees to the Begum, 4 months' pay to the rebels, 15 guns and his personal presence with the Army.'[55] Man Singh was agreeable to the first three terms but could not accept the last clause. The rebels declared war on him; burnt his villages and attacked the fort to breach it.[56] The battle lasted for a month and a half and over a thousand lives were lost. The fort was strong enough to withstand the attack and the rebels withdrew when they got news that the British troops were advancing on Faizabad.[57]

Man Singh was not the only taluqdar to face the wrath of the rebels. The raja of Tiloi was similarly invested by the rebels for twenty-six days without any succour from the British. In utter despair, he wrote to the Barrow, a British officer: '. . . I feel in great dismay, like a fish out of water, twisting round in distraction . . . I shall now perish. The whole country is against my life, and no one helps me . . . Your name is the cause of all my misery.' He had to sue for terms with the *nazim* of Salon.[58] Rustam Sah of Dera in Sultanpur had his estates confiscated by orders from Hazrat Mahal for siding with the British. Most importantly, the raja of Balrampur, Britain's strongest ally in Awadh, was threatened by Hazrat

Mahal with the support of taluqdars, the Nana and a force of 12,000 men.[59] Friends of the British were shown no mercy by the rebels under the leadership of Hazrat Mahal.

At this stage of the rebellion, the trans-Gogra region was where Hazrat Mahal's presence was most visible. The entire territory of the districts of Gonda and Bahraich was outside British control till late 1858. The rajas of Gonda and Churda remained staunchly with Hazrat Mahal and she was supported by Nana and Bala Rao, who had come in from Kanpur. Hazrat Mahal was ensconced in the fort of Baundi in Bahraich district with a strong force to support her: '. . . A force is encamped on all sides of the Fort, numbering about 15 or 16,000 including followers. Among these, there are 1500 cavalry and 500 mutineer sepoys, the rest are nujeebs and followers. There are also about 60 or 70 *shutre sowars* [soldiers on camels] . . . and 17 guns; 13 are outside the Fort of which only 5 are large.'[60] Hazrat Mahal, as we have noted already, issued orders to plunder those taluqdars who were showing loyalty to the British and to have their estates plundered. Even though the signs of retreat and disarray were becoming apparent, Hazrat Mahal's camp in northern Awadh continued to function as the seat of decision-making.

Through the pressure of fighting and because of all the deaths that had occurred in battle, matters had taken a different turn; new people replaced the old, new groups formed around Hazrat Mahal. It was now no longer possible to hold court. But there was still a decision-making body and Birjis Qadr was still the legitimizing authority—more so after the removal of Bahadur Shah in Delhi. Birjis Qadr was the legitimizing figure, behind whom was Hazrat Mahal. A man called Syed Abdul Hakim, who worked as an extra assistant in the British bureaucracy, was taken prisoner by the insurgents. On his release, he provided an account of the setup in Baundi.[61] This report said that orders were issued under the name of Birjis Qadr and collections were received by him from nazims and *chakladars* (revenue officials in charge of a fixed region, *chakla*, under Nawabi administration) appointed by him. Mumoo Khan acted as the agent but with him there was a coadjutor, Bakht Khan, a subahadar of artillery from Bareilly. The informant felt that there were elements of tension, rivalry and suspicion between the sepoys led by Bakht Khan and members of Hazrat Mahal's camp. Most of the time, Syed Abdul Hakim noted, it was Bakht Khan who called the shots. There existed another body, which was referred to by Hakim as 'the Parliament', and this body discussed and conducted all business. It consisted of the following persons: Maulavi Fuzl Huq, a former *serishtadar* (head officer in a court) in Delhi, who was always 'most violent in preaching a crusade against the British'; Maulavi Mahomed Hussian, formerly employed in the district of Agra; Kasim Ali; Raja Imdad Ali Khan of Kuntoor; Maulavi Ahmad Hussain; and Hakim Hussain, Raja of Bilgaon. Hakim added that 'these men (were) bitter in their hostility to the Government and spread the most absurd and incredible of reports.'

There are a few other points in this report that are worth noting. For one thing, the predominance of religious men marks a shift from what prevailed in Lucknow, where taluqdars like Jai Lal Singh and former ministers like Shurfuddaulah were most important. Also noteworthy is the fact that everyone in 'the Parliament' was Muslim. It is not impossible that these Islamic religious leaders used their hold over the populace to stir up anti-British feeling and whip up the flagging zeal. It is also ironic that Hazrat Mahal, who was opposed and defied by a maulavi in Lucknow, now found herself being advised by a group of six people of which three were maulavis. Perhaps the most intriguing part of Hakim's testimony is the mention of Bakht Khan and the critical role he played in decision-making. It is safe to assume that this was the same Bakht Khan who had been at the forefront of the battles in Delhi and who, after the defeat of the rebels there, had pleaded with Bahadur Shah to go with him to Lucknow.[62] Had Bahadur Shah accepted Khan's offer, his fate would probably have been different, and his presence in Lucknow might have added a new dimension to the rebellion. But such speculation apart, Bakht Khan's presence in the camp of Hazrat Mahal points to the interconnectedness of the various theatres of the uprising, as well as the role played by soldiers in decision-making.

In spite of these various groups, everything—the chain of command, the organization of forces, the battle order and tactical decisions—depended on the sanction of Birjis Qadr, i.e., Hazrat Mahal. In late September 1858, plans were drawn up for a coordinated movement of rebel forces throughout Awadh and northern and eastern Rohilkhand. At the risk of breaking the narrative, this plan demands to be quoted *in extenso*, if only to bear witness to the level of organization and planning that existed. The plan went as follows:

> Intizam-ood-Dowlah [translator's note: This I suppose is the title of Khan Ali Khan] is requested to concentrate a sufficient force including artillery for the defence of Pilibheet on the Bheera and Jugdawpoor roads. The leaders to be Enayet Ali Khan, Wuzeer Ali Khan . . . Intizam-ood-Dowlah is also requested to form a force for the taking

of Shahjehanpoor and Pourayan, under the command of General Ismael Khan and Mohsun Ali Khan. Intizam-ood-Dowlah will with the remaining troops and guns at his disposal, and the assistance of of talookdars and zemindars, guard the Sookutta Nullah and when required reinforce the troops at Pilibheet and Shahjehanpoor and look to the provision of supplies for them. Mohomed Soorabz Khan . . . and Mahomed-ood-Dowlah Bahadoor to proceed with troops under their command to the boundary of Pilibheet between the Dedah and to form an entrenchment at Billia Putwara. Enayet Khan, Amil of Sandee, Moulvie Fuzzul Huqq and Kashif Ali to be posted at Shahbad to interrupt the communication between Shahjehanpoor and Futtehghur. Mahomed Wallie Beg Khan, amil of Bangur, to stop the crossing of the British troops over the Ganges from Moorwaa Ghat to Nanamow Ghat. Raja Hurpershad Bahadoor to station his forces at Mohoriah Sewchuleea in the Baree Elaqua, for the collection of Khyrabad revenue and to check the advance of British troops from Bukshee Ki Talao and Mundeeaon, Mahomed Imad-ool-deen Khan Bahadur, Rajah Goolab Singh Bahadoor, Rajah Narpat Singh Bahadoor to form 4 detachments under their respective commands to be detached to Sundeela and the other two in the direction of Mulliabad and Ruheemabad. Valait Ahmed Amil at Sufeepoor and Chowdhree amil of Rasoolabad with the assistance of Talookdars and zemindars to form 2 parties, one to march towards Rasoolabad and the other to Oonam. Rana Beni Madho Buksh Dilare Jung, and Mahomed Fuzl Azeem Khan Bahadoor with the aid of Talookdars and troops at their disposal both foot and artillery to protect the borders of Oudh at the boundaries of Allahabad, Sooraon and Secundra sending half their force to reinforce the Nazim (of) Sultanpoor. Rugonath Singh Talookdar of Koree and Sindowlee, Rajah Dirg Bijah Singh Talookdar of Murarmow, Juggurnath Singh Talookdar of Sihiree, the wife of Bussunt Singh Talookdar of Simerpaha and Rugver Singh Collector with half their force to watch the Ghats of the Ganges within the district of Cawnpore and prevent the crossing of the British troops and with the remaining half meet British troops at Bunnee Buthura and Lucknow. Mahomed Sultan Hosein Chuckladar of Hydergurh and the Talookdars and zemindars of Hydergurh, also Hidayit Ali amil of Goorshaiganj etc. to concentrate their forces and attack Lucknow from the direction of Mahomed Bagh, Syud Mahdu Hossein Khan Bahadoor, Rajah Ali Buksh Khan Bahadur Talookdar of Rahona and Raja Madho Singh Bahadoor, Mahomed Hussun Khan Bahadoor, Talookdar of Bijowgarh, Goolab Singh, Talookdar of Narwal, Rajah Hosein Ali Khan, Ramsurroup Talookdar of Khera Deeah to attack the troops at Sooltanpoor and to hold the district from Pertabghur and Tandah. Moo Kurrif-ood-Dowlah Bahadoor and Rajah Dabee Buksh Singh Bahadoor . . . to attack Fyzabad and Amorodah and prevent the passage of troops within these respective boundaries. Hazim Hossein Khan with the men he has collected and the assistance of Talookdars of Kawary and others will protect the Ghats of the Ghogra with one fourth of their men, half the entire force to cross and attack Durriabad. Mahomed Dara Khan, Marka Salar [translator's note: chief of war] with his troops including artillery and Ahsan Ali Khan General and Goolam Abas, Naib Chukladar of Durriabad to attack

Durriabad. Moosahib Ali Khan Bahadoor and Akher Alee
with their respective troops including artillery, to attack
the British at Nawabganj from the direction of Sutrick and
Jalliapara. Raja Dirgbejae Sing, Talookdar of Mahonah,
Gholam Hosein Khan commanding the Abassee Regiment
and Hafiz Soorab Ali, tehseeldar to station their troops at
Mahonah near Bakshi-ki-Taloa and to hold the position
for the purpose of interrupting the line of communication.
Mahomed Yusuf Ali Khan Sipah Salar, General Mahomed
Hamid Khan, Khoda Bukx Khan Bahadoor, Rajah Goorbux
Sing, Ghoolam Russool Karindah of Ameerood Dowlah,
Ameer Hussein Khan Bahadoor, Mahomed Ali Khan
Bahadoor, Collector Mahomed Abdool Malee, Collector
and Reenut Sing Tallokdar of Thahanee to concentrate
their forces and attack Nawabgunge Bara Bunkee . . . [63]

This long extract is impressive not just because of the details
it commands but also because of the scale and range of the
planning that went into the deployment of troops. Obviously,
there were many people—nawabi officials, religious leaders,
minor princes, sepoys, taluqdars and their retainers and
zamindars—who were hostile to the British in September
1858 and were willing to take to arms and risk their lives to
fight them. There was the belief that a concerted and planned
attack would be enough to block the advance of the British
force under Campbell. Hazrat Mahal and her advisers also
believed that this diverse group of people would accept her
orders and respect her authority. It would be farfetched to
assume that these plans for deployment were worked out by
Hazrat Mahal alone. There was obviously a team—in today's
parlance, a think-tank or a council of war—that thought this

plan through. It shows a detailed knowledge of the geography of Awadh and also of who had authority in which part of the countryside, and in many cases, the number of troops or people a leader could command. This document throws light on another dimension of the rebellion to which the late C.A. Bayly first drew attention to in an original book.[64] He showed that just as the British used different modes of communication and information-gathering—from telegraph to the *harakara* and of course, Indian spies—to facilitate their counterinsurgency operations, the rebels on their part also displayed a remarkable awareness of the importance of communication, using lookouts and probably spies as well. This document shows not only the importance the rebel leadership placed on communication, or even on cutting of the communication lines of the British, but also the meticulous nature of the endeavour.

There are also very good reasons not to harbour the idea that these plans were mere figments of fantasy on the part of Hazrat Mahal and other leaders of the uprising. According to a British dispatch, 'Many of the movements have been made and foiled.'[65] As a follow-up to these orders, Beni Madho, the major figure of the resistance in southern Awadh,[66] fought Lieutenant Chamberlain and Major Bulwer in the vicinity of Purwa. He had 10,000 men and was forced to retreat only after five hours of fighting.[67] Similar in origin was Harprashad's crossing of the Gomti in early October with 12,000 men and twelve guns; he was assisted by several zamindars. Together this army attacked Sandila and took partial possession of the town for four days before he was forced to retreat. Harprashad's advance was the signal for Mansab Ali and Wilayat Ahmed to move from Banarmau and

Miangunj for a combined attack. They too were forced to retreat when they faced stiff British opposition.

Campbell (or Lord Clyde as he had become) opened his campaign in Awadh in the middle of October 1858. The plan was to deal with the rebels south of the Gogra in two simultaneous actions with the Lucknow-Kanpur road acting as the east-west divide. Rebels on both sides of the divide were to be driven across the Gogra. At the same time, British troops would move in from Rohilkhand in the west and Azamgarh in the east in two flanking movements. And another force would move into Awadh from the southern side. The impact of this massive manoeuvre would enable Lord Clyde to herd the rebels into the Nepal Terai. The outcome was achieved but not without fierce resistance, which took almost two months to quell and re-establish British authority across Awadh.[68] This time around, unlike what happened in February 1856, Awadh had to be conquered through a military campaign. Hazrat Mahal, whose former husband had agreed to surrender his kingdom but had refused to give up his dignity[69], fled to Nepal with 1500 followers. That was the swan song of the revolt in Awadh.

*

The rebellion in Jhansi, having broken out in a very dramatic manner with the massacre of the white population, lost momentum once the sepoys left for Delhi on 11 and 12 June. Lakshmibai's immediate response, as we saw in the previous chapter, was to write to Erskine to express her dependence on the British and to inform him that she was doing her best to keep the administration of Jhansi running to prevent the district from descending into lawlessness and chaos. In his reply, Erskine asked Lakshmibai 'to collect the Revenue, to raise Police and to do everything in her power to restore order' and said 'that accounts [would] be settled with her when Officers reach(ed) Jhansee . . .'[70] He enclosed a proclamation addressed to all the inhabitants of Jhansi. It said: 'Until Officers and Troops reach Jhansee, the Ranee will rule in the name of the British Government and I hereby call on all, great and small, to obey the Ranee, and to pay the Government Revenue to her for which they will receive credit.'[71] In the absence of British rule in Jhansi, Lakshmibai was being asked to be its surrogate. In these initial stages of the rebellion in Jhansi, she did not defy British rule; on the contrary, she worked as its representative. There was an element of continuity in this since the ruling house of Jhansi had existed first at the behest of the Peshwas and then of the British, who had bestowed on them the status of royalty.

This correspondence between Lakshmibai and the representative of British rule in Central India needs to be read with the letter she wrote to the ruler of Datia. In that letter, after having narrated what had transpired in Jhansi, she appealed to all chiefs to make a combined attempt 'to check the disturbances'. Later she met representatives from Datia and Orcha and told them that 'till arrangements were made from Jabalpur (by the British) such measures should be taken at Jhansi that no disturbances would occur.'[72] This only reinforces the point that Lakshmibai was acting on behalf of the British and awaiting their arrival.

Collecting revenue and establishing authority, as Lakshmibai anticipated, turned out to be full of difficulties and opposition. After Gangadhar Rao's death, one claimant to the title had been Sadashiv Rao of Parola, 'a nephew many times removed', according to Sen. He saw a chance again when British authority collapsed, and he gathered troops and seized the fort of Karera, about thirty miles from Jhansi. He drove out the police and the revenue officials and continued to create disturbances in the neighbouring villages. Lakshmibai sent a force to drive him out of Karera but Sadashiv Rao, now styling himself as Maharaja, retreated to Narwar, which was in the territories belonging to Sindhias. There he collected an army and again began harassing Lakshmibai, who had him captured and kept as a prisoner in the fort at Jhansi. (He was later executed by the British).[73] The opposition from Sadashiv Rao was a minor irritant compared to what Lakshmibai faced from the Bundelas, who considered the Marathas to be interlopers in their territory. When the Bundela chieftains found Jhansi without British protection, they decided to move in. Sen provides the following account based on that of the late nineteenth-century writer Parasnis. The diwan of Orcha, Nathe Khan, decided to invade Jhansi, but before that, he offered Lakshmibai the same pension as the British, provided she surrender her kingdom. When the Orcha army invaded Jhansi—the dates are unclear—Lakshmibai had very few troops and even fewer military resources. She appealed to the feudal lords in her territories, who rallied behind her even though many of them were Bundelas. She suffered early setbacks and Nathe Khan and his army came right up to the walls of the fort. It is said that at this juncture Lakshmibai appeared for the first time before her troops and the Orcha troops were repulsed. Even the Raja of Datia entered the fray, having made an agreement with the ruler of Orcha to divide Jhansi between them.[74] Much later, in January 1858, in a letter to Robert Hamilton, Lakshmibai informed him about her situation of the previous year after the sepoys had risen in revolt and she had assumed charge:

> Taking advantage of the disturbed state of the country, the chiefs of Dutya and Orcha first took possession of the district of Jhansee Illaka that lay on the borders of their respective states, both to the East and West. On the 3rd September (both these chiefs acting in concert) the Forces of Oorcha composed of the Thakoors and relations of the State, and amounting to 40,000 men and 28 Guns invaded Jhansi itself and made other Chiefs support them . . . I tried my best by selling my property, taking money on interest, collected a party of men and took steps to protect the city and to meet the invading force. The enemy by firing guns, matchlocks and rockets [some word that is illegible] did much mischief and killed thousands of precious souls. My resources failing, I wrote on the 20th September and 19th October for reinforcements. After two months the besieging force retired to a village ... situated about 3 miles from Orcha. All the districts that were formerly occupied by the chief of Orcha are still in his possession. In the same manner the ranee of Datya still holds all the districts that fell into her hands. The authorities at Orcha and Datya do not give up these places, the troop sent to reoccupy them met with opposition. As was the case in former days, the sowars and the mawasas are excited to ruin by rapine and plunder the remaining districts.[75]

Looking back on the events between June and December 1857, Lakshmibai made herself out to be a victim of violence, first of the sepoys and then of the Bundela chiefs, and in desperate need of protection and rescue by the British. Parasnis, the Marathi writer referred to earlier, wrote that the Union Jack was displayed on the Jhansi fort during this period.[76]

Lakshmibai's position through the second half of 1857 remained precarious and complicated. On the one hand, she wished to establish her authority in Jhansi to affirm her own commitment to it and her *izzat*, or to show the British that she was someone who could be trusted. The latter is certainly what she wanted to convey. But circumstances to do with the momentum and the fate of the rebellion were spinning out of her control and running against her. One British report filed from Indore some 300 kilometres away from Jhansi noted, 'The Ranee of Jhansie continues to rule Jhansie. All disaffected and mutinous men that go to Jhansie are kept by the Ranee . . . Although the news of the total defeat of the rebels at Cawnpore and that of the advance of the British forces has been received by the Ranee she seems to entertain no fears. The Thakoors all persuade her that Europeans are not to be found in India, and by giving about such reports they serve their own ends, and make the lady pay them thousands of rupees.'[77]

The sentence—'All disaffected and mutinous men that go to Jhansie are kept by the Ranee'—is of some importance. As the rebels suffered reversals in the different centres of north India, especially in places like Kanpur, Gwalior, Allahabad, and so on, they sought refuge in places that were outside British control. Large groups of them went to Awadh and other groups to Bundelkhand, especially to Jhansi, where Lakshmibai appeared to be holding sway. They came to

Jhansi to continue the rebellion, but they also came in search of food and livelihood. What could Lakshmibai do with this population that was coming into Jhansi? It was not within her power to throw them out. Neither could she completely disregard them. Without food and income, this population would turn disorderly and take to loot and plunder, which would seriously undermine her authority. She chose to employ them—hence the statement in the report '[they] are kept by the Ranee.' The British, as the report suggests, saw Lakshmibai's actions in a completely different light—as evidence that she was gathering men to resist the British. Lakshmibai was caught between popular pressure around her and the suspicions of the British.

To understand the attitude of the British towards Lakshmibai, it is necessary to go back to the correspondence she had with Erskine. In his reply the latter said: 'When Officers reach Jhansee . . . she will be liberally dealt with.'[78] But the Governor General did not give his unconditional approval to Erskine's decision, especially the promise to deal liberally with Lakshmibai. The Secretary to the Government of India officially informed Erskine that if her version of events proved to be false, she would not be protected. The letter added, 'From the account supplied to Government by Major Ellis it appears that the Ranee did lend assistance to the mutineers and rebels, and that she gave guns and men.'[79] In the eyes of the British, prone to seeing everything at the time of insurgency in black and white and as either loyalty or rebellion, any sympathy for someone who had assisted the rebels was out of the question. The notion that Lakshmibai was *compelled* to provide 'guns and men' was not of any relevance. As events moved, this conviction gained ground and was aggravated by the possibility that she had been involved in the massacre of sixty white men, women and children in Jhansi in early June 1857. In Sen's words, 'Jhansi called for vengeance and the victim had to be a person of sufficient importance.'[80] Who other than Lakshmibai quite fit the bill of 'sufficient importance' in Jhansi?

At some point in late 1857, Lakshmibai was pointedly asked by Bukhshish Ali, the former *daroga* of the jail in Jhansi, if she would fight the British. It is not possible to put a precise date to this incident, which was reported to the British on or before 8 January. According to the report, she replied that she would not fight the British and would 'return all the districts under her to the British officers when they (came) to Jhansee.'[81] Yet she ensured that the cavalry was well-trained; that three to four mounds of gunpowder (for this purpose she had supplies of saltpetre brought in from Gwalior)[82] were manufactured every day and stored in the fort; four old guns were repaired and five new ones were produced. She had an army of 400 of her own forces, as well as men belonging to the thakurs.[83] Many of the soldiers who were present in Jhansi refused to come to terms with the British. Hasan Ali Khan, the rissaldar and other officers made it clear to Lakshmibai that if she was not prepared to oppose the British, they should be relieved of their services and their outstanding salaries paid.[84] There was thus considerable pressure on her to resist the British. But she continued to assert that she would not fight them. In fact, in her letter to Hamilton written on 1 January 1858, she lamented the fact that the British were not coming forward to help and protect her. Without that help and protection, she believed she was ruined. She wrote:

Under the circumstances I can never expect to get rid of these enemies and to clear myself of the heavy debts without the assistance of the British government. The Commissioner seems not prepared to move for myself as he states in his letter dated 9th November that the services of the British troops for the present are required at his quarter. As these short-sighted individuals seem unmindful of the British supremacy and do their best to ruin myself and the whole country I beg you will give me your support in the best way you can and thus save myself and all the people who are reduced to the last extremity, and are not able to cope with the enemy.[85]

Lakshmibai's position became precarious, if not non-viable, from around the beginning of February 1858 when British counter-insurgency forces under General Hugh Rose began operations in Bundelkhand. By the 15th of February he had occupied Sagar and decided to move north to Jhansi. Rebel forces were stationed in various places to stop Rose's advance.[86] Either by defeating or bypassing these pockets of resistance, Rose besieged Jhansi on 21 March. The information that the British had regarding Lakshmibai at this juncture was based on reports like the following sent in by one Ganesh Lal, the Indian superintendent based temporarily in Datia: 'The Baee of Jhansi no doubt is preparing herself to fight against us. She has filled the Jhansi fort with supplies, ammunition, good large old and newly-made guns etc. She is very bold . . . She is clearing and cutting down all the trees etc. around the fort and around the walls of the town.'[87] Furthermore, certain proclamations had been circulating in Bundelkhand inciting people in the name of religion (both Hinduism and Islam) to fight and destroy the British. They went around in Jhansi, too, and from this the British concluded that these were ishtahars that had been put out by Lakshmibai herself. This, together with the growing conviction that she was involved, if not responsible, for the massacre of the British in Jhansi, nullified all her written protestations of loyalty. In the eyes of the British, Lakshmibai was enemy numero uno.

The British assault on Jhansi began in earnest on 26 March. But success was not easy for Rose. Six guns had been placed on the walls of the city; all houses near the walls were evacuated so that soldiers could be positioned in them.[88] It was perhaps based on seeing such preparations that the following report by a spy was sent to the British: 'The Rani was both disposed to fight and to make terms, to fight from the fear of mutineers in her service, to make terms by the advice of some of her functionaries. But preparations are being made to fight.'[89] Lakshmibai did make desperate attempts to make peace with the British. She sent a letter to Rose and on 18 March she learnt from one of the harkaras that he had delivered the letter to the agent but had got no reply.[90] As Rose's assault began, Lakshmibai seemed to sink into despair. An intelligence report said, 'The Ranee did not take her meals till evening and was much distressed and distracted. She took up her quarters in an underground house in the Fort.'[91]

Outside the fort there were no signs of distress and despair. On learning that Rose's army was laying siege to Jhansi, Tantia Tope with his army set out for Jhansi with a plan to attack the British troops from the rear. On 31 March, he crossed the Betwa river located behind Rose's force. To signal to the rebels in Jhansi that they had arrived in the vicinity, Tantia Tope's men lit a huge bonfire on a hillock. The signal was greeted with shouts of joy and guns were fired from the city. Rose had now to fight the rebels who were constantly attacking from within the fort in front of him, as well as those who were attacking his rear. He managed to repulse and disperse the latter but not to defeat them.[92] It was only after this that Rose could concentrate his forces on Jhansi.

The resistance that Rose met from within the town and the fort was fierce. Rose reported: 'The attack on Jhansie offered serious difficulties. There was no way of breaching the Fort except from the South but the South was flanked by the fortified City wall . . .' Other reasons that made breaching the Fort difficult were spelt out thus by Rose:

> The great strength of the Fort, natural as well as artificial, and its extent, entitles it to a place amongst fortresses. It stands on an elevated rock, rising out of a plain, and commands the city, and surrounding country; it is built of excellent and most massive masonry. The Fort is difficult to breach, because, composed of granite, its walls vary in thickness from sixteen to twenty feet . . . The fortress is surrounded by the city of Jhansie on all sides, except the West and part of the South face. The steepness of the rock protects the West, the fortified city wall with bastions springing from the centre of its South face, running South, and ending in a high mound or mamelon, protects by a flanking fire on its South face. The mound was fortified by a strong circular bastion for 5 Guns, round part of which was drawn a ditch 12 feet deep and 15 feet broad of solid masonry. Quantities of men were always at work in the mound.[93]

The resistance was provided by an army that consisted of about 10,000 Bundelas and *vilayaties* (probably Afghans or even soldiers from the north), 1500 sepoys, of which 400 were sowars, and thirty to forty guns.[94] This combined force defended both the town and the fort. A tower called the White Turret had the advantage of height and it was armed heavily with several batteries positioned at strategic points. From here the British army was fired upon constantly. The fort of Jhansi, as Rose noted, had a natural line of defence, and this was strengthened by the rebel troops. Rose commented on the military skill involved in the resistance: 'The Chief of the Rebel Artillery was a first-rate Artillery-man; he had under him two Companies of Goolundauze. The manner in which the Rebels served their Guns, repaired their defences, and re-opened fire from batteries and Guns repeatedly shut up, was remarkable. From some batteries they returned shot for shot.'[95] In the same report, Rose made a very significant observation: 'The women were seen working in the batteries and carrying ammunition.'[96] To this, Sen, without citing a source, added: 'In the evening the Rani herself went round the defences to inspire her men with zeal and enthusiasm.'[97]

Having taken the Fort, Rose had to clear the town of Jhansi, where 'numerous armed Rebels . . . remained in the houses, and, who were firing on the troops.' The resistance within the town had a different dimension—somewhat similar to what Clydes's troops encountered in the lanes and alleys of Lucknow. Rose wrote that it involved:

> Bloody, often hand-to-hand, combats; one of the most remarkable of them was between detachments of Her Majesty's 85th Regiment and 3rd Europeans, and thirty or

forty Velaitie Sowars, the body-guard of the Ranee, in the Palace Stables under the fire of the Fort. The Sowars, full of opium, defended their Stables, firing with matchlocks and pistols from the windows and loop-holes, and cutting with their tulwars, and from behind the doors. When driven in they retreated behind their houses, still firing or fighting with their swords in both hands till they were shot or bayoneted struggling even when dying on the ground to strike again. A party of them remained in a room off the stables which was on fire till they were half burnt; their clothes in flames, they rushed out hacking at their assailants, and guarding their heads with their shields.[98]

The desperate nature of the fighting and the hatred of the British were illustrated by two incidents that Rose recorded: 'Numerous incidents marked the desperate feeling which animated the defenders. A retainer of the Ranee tried to blow up himself and his wife; failing in the attempt, he endeavoured to cut her to pieces and then killed himself. Two Vilaities, attacked by the videttes, threw a woman who was with them into a well, and then jumped down it themselves.'[99]

Hugh Rose's summing up of the nature of the resistance he faced is worth quoting: 'Everything indicated a general and determined resistance; this was not surprising, as the inhabitants, from the Ranee downwards, were, more or less, concerned in the murder and plunder of the English. There was hardly a house in Jhansie which did not contain some article of English plunder, and politically speaking, the Rebel confederacy knew well that if Jhansie, the richest Hindoo city, and most important fortress in Central India fell, the cause of the insurgents in this part of India fell also.'[100]

There are two points that are important in this assessment. One is the firm conviction that Lakshmibai, and almost the entire population of Jhansi, had the blood of the British on their hands. This was no longer a suspicion. This is the context of what happened in Jhansi once the rebels had been defeated. Second, it is evident from what Rose wrote, and his conclusion was based on the facts given in the previous paragraph, that the uprising in Jhansi—notwithstanding whatever might have been Lakshmibai's intentions and her declarations of loyalty to the British—had become a popular resistance against the British. She was swept into the folds of the rebellion.

The takeover of Jhansi by the British was marked by scenes similar to those seen in Lucknow in March 1858 when the British army entered that city. Killing and plunder motivated by vengeance and hatred reigned supreme. One writer noted, 'No maudlin clemency was to mark the fall of the city.'[101] No Indian, soldier or civilian, was spared: the colour of the skin was the sign of a rebel. The British troops became plunderers. The writer said that the soldiers smashed and destroyed everything they found. Another account was very graphic:

> . . . Soon as the fighting had ceased, officers and men began to look about them with that spirit of curiosity which pervades one when visiting the shops of Wardour Street, Leicester Square: they dived into every house and searched its dark corners, they pulled down walls, or parts of walls, which looked of recent build, all in this self-same spirit of curiosity . . . One class of articles, however, seemed to me to be looked on as fair loot . . . these were the gods found in

the temples. They were collected in great numbers, and were strangely sought after by every officer and soldier. There were Gunputties and Vishnoos innumerable, and of every metal. Some wore really pretty ornaments, silver, with gold bangles on their grotesque limbs, and small enough to be worn on the watch chain: others were of brass and stone, of rare workmanship.

A good many jewels were also pocketed. The famous library of Sanskrit manuscripts was totally destroyed.[102]

Hugh Rose successfully captured Jhansi, but he failed to capture his principal target, Lakshmibai. Rose reported that on the morning of 5 April, a wounded Maratha retainer of Lakshmibai brought before him informed him that on the previous night, she had escaped from Jhansi with 300 vilayatis and 25 sowars. Perhaps Lakshmibai's escape, like Hazrat Mahal's flight from Lucknow, was possible because in both places the avenging British armies had been more keen to loot and plunder than to capture the chief protagonists of the uprising. Rose ordered a section of his force to give chase; in the town of Bandiri, towards which Lakshmibai had fled, the British 'saw traces of the Ranee's hasty flight, and her tent in which was an unfinished breakfast'. The pursuers had a glimpse of her on a grey horse riding away with four attendants.[103] Lakshmibai had lost her Jhansi but she herself survived to fight the British for two more months.

Free of her pursuers, Lakshmibai rode off towards Kalpi, still a rebel bastion, to join Tantia Tope. Rose was aware of the gathering of the rebels at Kalpi as a kind of last stand and also of the strategic importance of Kalpi. Rose noted:

Culpee, on the right bank of the Jumna, in the hands of the rebels, prevented the concentration of the British Armies of the West [Rose had come up from Bombay], with those of the East of India [i.e., the force under Lord Clyde]; exposed to attack, from the line of the Jumna, the Army engaged in operations against the insurgents in the Doab, the line of the Ganges; Oudh; and Rohilcund; and so long as Culpee was Rebel, so had it the enemy in their power to say that the East and West of India might be British, but that the pivot of its centre was theirs.[104]

Rose was not unaware of the importance of Kalpi nor was the rebel leadership. The nature of the resistance at Kalpi would demonstrate this awareness. Kalpi, Rose discovered as he neared it, had before it a 'labyrinth of ravines' and eighty-four temples. The rebels had cut deep trenches across the road; there was also another 'chain of ravines' between the town and the fort. The latter was protected on all sides by ravines and to the rear there was the Jamuna, from which rose 'the precipitous rock on which it (the fort) stands.'[105]

The rebels decided to resist Rose first at the town of Koonch—'an open town; but it is difficult to attack, because it is surrounded by woods, gardens, and temples, with high walls around them, every one of which is a defence.' Rebels moved in from Kalpi to Koonch and among them were 500 vilaytis under Lakshmibai.[106] After the setback at Koonch, these vilaytis felt it was their duty to escort Lakshmibai to a place of safety,[107] which presumably was Kalpi, where she was part of the resistance. The rebels were exhorted 'to hold to the last, Calpee their only arsenal, and to win their right to Paradise by exterminating the Infidel English.'[108] In Kalpi and its environs, the resistance that Rose encountered did not come only from soldiers and armed people, but unarmed common people also offered resistance. According to Rose:

> The inhabitants of the valley of the Jumna were the most disaffected my Force had yet met with. They had been under Rebel rule, and had never felt the influence of British Power since the commencement of the insurrection. Every village had its one or two Mahratta Pundits, who had made a most successful propaganda in favour of Nana Sahib as Peishwa. The villagers did good service to the Rebels, by betraying to them our Daks and movements, as well as some carts, when their drivers, on account of the exhausted state of their cattle, could not keep their place in the Column, or sought water at a distance from the road.[109]

The rebels offered a stiff resistance under the leadership of Rao Sahib, a nephew of Nana Sahib, the Nawab of Banda and Lakshmibai. The rebel army was composed of the Gwalior Contingent, comprising 'the finest men, best drilled and organized Native Troops of all arms in India'; other regiments of the Bengal Infantry; the rebel cavalry from Kotah; and a chosen band of vilayatis. This force was reinforced by the army of the Nawab of Banda, consisting of a number of men from the mutinous Bengal Cavalry, of which the 5th Irregulars in their red uniforms were conspicuous. That this force was disciplined and orderly was noticeable from the fact that 'all the Sepoy Regiments kept up, carefully, their English equipment and organization; the words of command for drill, grand rounds &c, were given, as we could hear at night, in English.'[110] The rebel soldiers were thus fighting the British with the very discipline and military organization that they had learnt from the British. This force, Rose heard, 'had sworn a religious oath on the waters of the Jumna . . . that they would drive [the army under Rose] into the Jumna and destroy it, or die.'[111] All this ensured a stiff resistance to Rose but did not bring victory. The rebels escaped from Kalpi in groups to Gwalior, where Tantia Tope, much to everyone's surprise—and shock in the case of the British—had incited Sindhia's soldiers to mutiny. Rose marched to Gwalior, and it was in the defence of Gwalior that Lakshmibai was last sighted at the battle of Kotah-ka-Serai in the middle of June. The first report of her death was unadorned and without any details: 'The Ranee of Jhansee also lost her life in the melee.'[112] Lakshmibai died fighting.

*

The rebellions in Lucknow and Jhansi followed different trajectories, even though in both places the revolt began around the same time: only a week separated the two mutinies. They ended, however, at different times. The uprising in Lucknow spilled over into the Awadh countryside in October 1857 and could only be quelled completely in November 1858. The revolt in Awadh lasted well over a year. The rebellion in Jhansi, while short-lived, also spread into the countryside once Jhansi fell and Lakshmibai escaped in early April. Battles were fought in Koonch, Kalpi and near Gwalior, but with the exception of a few dying embers, the fire went out of the resistance completely following Lakshmibai's death and the capture of Gwalior by the British. What is important as a point of contrast is that in Jhansi, unlike in Lucknow, the rebellion was not continuous. Once the sepoys rode off towards Delhi and Lakshmibai assumed the administration of Jhansi, there was no one left to resist. In Lucknow, on the other hand, the remnants of British rule remained in the shape of those who were trapped in the Residency atop which the Union Jack still fluttered. The first stage of the revolt in Lucknow was an attempt to dislodge the British from the Residency and to take over that symbol of British power. This fight continued in Lucknow after Havelock and Campbell's 'relief' before spreading into rural Awadh. In Jhansi, resistance to the British began as Rose's force approached it in late March and besieged the fort and the town. Though fierce, it was not long-drawn and ended by early April. Beyond Jhansi, the resistance was over by end June. In both places the rebellion acquired the character of a popular resistance, but their duration and intensity were different.

The nature of participation of Hazrat Mahal and Lakshmibai was also different. Hazrat Mahal became a rebel and leading figure almost as soon as the rebellion began in Lucknow. Lakshmibai, on the other hand, initially kept her distance from the mutiny and the massacre in Jhansi, even declaring her loyalty to the British, seeking their protection and claiming to rule Jhansi on their behalf. She turned a rebel much later and through a very different process. She was forced to embrace the revolt not only because the pressure from the rebels mounted, but also because she realized that the British were not going to come to her aid. In their eyes, she was no more than a figure of suspicion and loathing. The type of leadership each of the two women provided was also different. There is no evidence that Hazrat Mahal ever went into battle—she planned, gave orders and tried to rouse the rebels to keep on fighting. She was like the general at the back of the battleground, rather than in the thick of the gun-smoke of war. Lakshmibai was quite the opposite. Once she turned a rebel, she joined the uprising as an actual warrior. In battle, she led from the front. In this context, the circumstances of their deaths were apposite. Hazrat Mahal, escaping capture at the hands of Lord Clyde's troops, fled to Nepal and died there in penury. Lakshmibai embraced a soldier's death. This probably enhanced her charisma in the eyes of the British and of subsequent generations.

LEADERSHIP

The revolt of 1857 was, of course, a war of arms. It was also a war of words. What the rebels had to say for themselves was invariably articulated by the leadership. Most of the rebels—sepoys, peasants, artisans, common people—had no access to the gifts of reading and writing. Moreover, they were too involved in the life-and-death struggle that the rebellion called for. They left the war of words to the leaders. It is not that the sepoy or the peasant was always silent; we will have occasion to turn to what some of them did say, when they could. The rebel leadership spoke through various ishtahars, pamphlets, hukumnamahs and so on. In one remarkable instance, as already noted and quoted, a rebel taluqdar—Hanwant Singh of Kalakankar—voiced his grievances and aims to a British officer to whom he had given shelter. These expressions from the rebel leaders offer a rare glimpse into the mind of the rebellion: what drove them, why they rebelled, what they wanted to achieve and so on. The rebellion is far too often seen, by historians of different persuasions, to be devoid of a mind or a consciousness. But it had a mind or perhaps several minds.

These expressions also help to understand distinct styles of leadership. This chapter attempts to address some of these issues through what Hazrat Mahal and Lakshmibai had to say or did not have to say. The voices of some other leaders will occasionally enter the discussion.

In Awadh, the most significant battle in the war of words occurred rather late, when the rebellion was sounding its last post. The first volley was fired, not unexpectedly, by the British, and it came from the highest authority—Queen Victoria herself, in a proclamation dated 1 November 1858, announced that India would no longer be administered by the East India Company but would be ruled directly by the Crown. The proclamation had certain significant angles. In October 1857, immediately after the fall of Delhi, Lord Palmerston, the then prime minister, wrote to Queen Victoria about 'the inconvenience of administering the Govt of a vast country on the other side of the Globe by means of two Cabinets, the one responsible to your Majesty & to Parliament, the other only responsible to a mob of Holders of Indian stock, assembled for 3 or 4 hours, 3 or 4 times a year.'[1] This set in motion the process of preparing a bill to transfer power to the monarch and her ministers. This bill was finally finished and presented to the queen and parliament by Lord Derby, who became prime minister after Palmerston and his colleagues resigned in February 1858. The next step was to announce this change in India, to Indians. Lord Derby decided to do this through a proclamation in the words of the queen, who would speak directly to her new subjects. The basic features of the announcement were straightforward: the Crown was to assume direct authority; the Governor General would be renamed Viceroy; all existing treaties with native rulers were to be accepted; public services would be open to Indians and Europeans; equal and impartial protection was to be given to all subjects in the exercise of religion and in the maintenance of property rights; and there would be an amnesty. When the draft was presented to Queen Victoria, she did not approve it and said that the proclamation 'must be almost entirely remodelled.' She objected to the tone and the content. She asked for all references to the British government to be changed to the royal 'we'. More importantly, on the question of religious neutrality, she wanted it said that since she was deeply attached to her own religion, she would not interfere with the religion of the Indian people. The changes were mostly incorporated. But there is one point on which the actual proclamation differed from what the queen had proposed. There was no mention that Indians would enjoy the same equality as the other subjects of the British Crown. The closest thought to that promise appeared in the seventh paragraph, where it was declared that the Queen would 'hold Ourselves bound to the Natives of Our Indian Territories by the same obligations of Duty which bind Us to all our other Subjects.'[2] The Queen's Proclamation was announced in India on 1 November and simultaneously translated into all Indian languages.

One such translation, either an Urdu or a Persian one, must have reached Hazrat Mahal and her entourage. Even though she was busy fighting and retreating before the advancing British columns, she issued a counter proclamation in the name of Birjis Qadr.[3] This proclamation—the Begum's Proclamation as it is often called—was 'extensively circulated, not only through the distant provinces of Oudh, but even in the capital itself.'[4] Most importantly, what this proclamation articulated was the deep-seated mistrust that the rebels had for the British and whatever they said. The anonymous author of the Begum's proclamation took up one by one the announcements and the promises of the Queen's proclamation and attacked them, tearing them to shreds. Nothing that Queen Victoria said or promised should or could be believed, Hazrat Mahal said, adding that British rule in India was an act of bad faith.

Each and every issue that was discussed began with the tag line, 'It is written in the proclamation' or a variation of this, 'In the proclamation it is written . . .' The Begum's proclamation began with the announcement that henceforth Hindustan would be ruled by the queen and her laws would have to be obeyed. It said that before this announcement Hindustan had been 'held in trust by the Company'. To counter this 'change' that was taking place, the Begum's proclamation said, 'for the laws of the Company, the settlement of the Company, the English servants of the Company, the Governor General, and the judicial administration of the Company, are all unchanged.' Hazrat Mahal (or if not the Begum herself, the person who drafted the proclamation) was quick to latch on to the fact that the shift from the Company to the Crown was only nominal and not a substantive change. In reality, the British government had been ruling India all along. The Begum's reply underlined this point by noting that the Company only held Hindustan 'in trust'. The point is significant because way back in 1858, the rebel leadership had understood a reality that some historians (mostly British) still continue to deny.

The second point that the Begum's proclamation took up for rebuttal was the Queen's promise that her reign would accept all the treaties made by the Company with the Indian powers, princes etc. The Begum labelled this promise an 'artifice' and went on to ask the very valid question: 'The Company has seized on the whole of Hindoostan, and, if this arrangement be accepted, what is there new in it?' It went on to narrate how many—if not all—instances of annexation made by the British were, in fact, acts of betrayal. The proclamation asserted that the Company professed to treat the ruler of Bharatpur as a son and under this pretext took over his territories. The 'chief of Lahore'—presumably meaning Dalip Singh—was taken to London and 'it has not fallen to his lot to return.' The Peshwa was expelled from Poona but held as a prisoner in Bithur. It continued, '. . . their breach of faith with Sultan Tippoo is well known; the Rajah of Benares they imprisoned in Agra. Under pretence of administering the country of the Chief of Gwalior, they introduced English customs; they have left no names or traces of the Chiefs of Behar, Orissa and Bengal; they gave the Rao of Furruckabad a small allowance, and took his territory.' On the treatment of the nawabs of Awadh, the proclamation began by listing the areas that Wellesley seized from the nawab in 1801—Shahjahanpur, Bareilly, Azimgarh, Jaunpur, Gorakhpur, Etawah, Allahabad, Fatehpur etc.—then adding: 'Our ancestral possessions they took from us on pretence of distributing pay; and in the 7th article of the treaty they wrote, on oath, that they would take no more from us.' An important question was raised: 'If, then, the arrangements made by the Company are to be accepted, what is the difference between the former and the present state of things?' The proclamation turned from what it called 'old affairs' to more recent events in which 'in defiance of treaties and oaths, and notwithstanding that they owed us millions of rupees, without reason, and on pretence of the misconduct and discontent of our people, they took our country and property, worth millions of rupees.'

Having raised the premise of Lord Dalhousie's annexation of Awadh—the persistent misgovernment by the nawabs—the proclamation asked a very valid question: If the people were genuinely discontented with Wajid Ali Shah, how could they be happy with his successor? The proclamation claimed for Birjis Qadr and Hazrat Mahal the following: 'No ruler ever experienced such loyalty and devotion of life and goods as we have done.' On the basis of such expressions of loyalty Awadh should be restored to its rightful ruler—'If the Queen has assumed the government, why does Her Majesty not restore our country to us when our people wish it?'

The Begum's proclamation proceeded to address the thorny issue of religious toleration. It began by first citing what the Queen had said in her proclamation: '. . . It is written that the Christian religion is true but that no other creed will suffer oppression, and that the laws will be observed towards all.' The proclamation's criticism of this statement began with a very fundamental question, which resonates even today. 'What has the administration of justice to do with the truth or falsehood of religion?' It went on to launch an attack on Christian religious beliefs and practices by asserting that only that religion which acknowledges one God is true; but the religion which recognizes three Gods cannot be accepted as true by anybody—'neither Mussulman nor Hindoo—nay, not even Jews, Sun-worshippers, or Fire-worshippers can believe it true.' It is significant, and this is a point to which we will return later in the discussion, that the proclamation was willing to see the practices of Hindus as monotheistic but the Christian doctrine of the Trinity as polytheistic.

From doctrine the proclamation shifted its focus to policies pursued by the British government in India. This was a no-holds barred attack: 'To eat pigs and drink wine—to bite greased cartridges, and to mix pig's fat with flour and sweetmeats—to destroy Hindoos and Mussalman temples on pretence of making roads to build churches—to send clergymen into the streets and alleys to preach the Christian religion—to institute English schools, and to pay a monthly stipend for learning the English sciences, while the places of worship of Hindoos and Mussalmans are to this day entirely neglected; with all this, how can the people believe that religion will not be interfered with?' This attack on many of the features of the age of reform inaugurated by Bentinck and Macaulay from the 1830s was followed by a statement on the motivation of the rebellion: 'The rebellion began with religion, and for it, millions of men have been killed. Let not our subjects be deceived; thousands were deprived of their religion in the North-West, and thousands were hanged rather than abandon their religion.'

The proclamation thus puts out two driving forces of the uprising: one was the threat to the religious beliefs and practices of both Muslims and Hindus, exacerbated by the menace of conversion, either directly through churches and padres, or at times covertly, by introducing polluting agents into foodstuff. The other was the loyalty shown by the people towards the line of Wajid Ali Shah, which directly points to the act of betrayal that the annexation of Awadh represented. All this connected to the larger matter that the British were not trustworthy. By extension, therefore, the Queen's Proclamation could not be trusted.

As its concluding volley, the Begum's proclamation addressed the issue of the treatment of the rebels by the Crown. The Queen's proclamation promised that the lives of those who had sheltered rebels, provided leadership to them, or had caused men to rebel would be saved 'but that punishment shall be awarded after deliberation, and that murderers and abettors of murderers shall have no mercy shown them, while all others shall be forgiven.' The Begum's stand on this: 'Any foolish person can see, that under this proclamation no one, be he guilty or innocent, can escape.' The charge was that the British were being disingenuous: 'Everything is written, and yet nothing is written . . . they have clearly written that they will not let off any one implicated; and in whatever village or estate the army may have halted, the inhabitants of that place cannot escape.' The announcement bearing the seal of Queen Victoria 'teems with enmity'. And it warned those who were being taken in by this apparent promise of pardon that 'no one [had] ever seen in a dream that the English forgave an offence.'

The Queen's Proclamation had promised an expansion of public works to improve the condition of the people of India. The Begum retorted, 'It is worthy of little reflection, that they have promised no better employment for Hindoostanees than making roads and digging canals. If people cannot see clearly what this means, there can be no help for them. Let no subject be deceived by the proclamation.'

The begum's arguments help clarify a few things. In spite of the hazards of war, at a time of retreat no less, Hazrat Mahal's team had devoted attention to the Queen's

Proclamation, reading it very closely and working out the implications of its various statements. This was in all likelihood not the work of one person. It probably involved a degree of collective thinking—perhaps Hazrat Mahal had formed a brain trust or a strategy group. Reading the Queen's document was not enough. It was important to formulate the most complete and convincing reply. The result of this is clear from even a cursory reading of the Begum's proclamation. It proceeds point by point or issue by issue, sharply and clearly, which was necessary given the purpose of the proclamation and the nature of its target audience. It was not written only as a rebuttal to Queen Victoria—in fact, the queen was not the main target—but more importantly to infuse zeal in the rebels so they could continue the war to defeat the firangi. It was addressed to the people of India, more specifically to those who had taken up arms to defy British rule. The Begum's proclamation thus operates on at least two different but interrelated registers. One was to attack the British, and through this attack, to demonstrate that the British were utterly untrustworthy. This was done through a reading of the history of British rule in India, which showed that the British had not kept their word with a single Indian ruler or prince. The establishment of British rule in India was a chronicle of broken promises and betrayal. The history of the relationship between the Awadh nawabs and the British was the most telling in this long narrative of perfidy. Having established their rule, the British had gone about destroying what the Indian people cherished most and had replaced it with roads, churches, schools etc. What the British policymakers thought of as gifts of civilization—the so-called burden of the white man—

was made into objects of attack. Everything connected with British rule became an item in a long list of grievances.

At another level, the Begum's proclamation was also an instrument of propaganda and persuasion. The proclamation wanted to convince the people that Indian rulers were better and kinder than the British: 'it is . . . necessary to remember that Hindoostanee rulers are altogether kind and merciful'. There was no need to prove this: 'Thousands have seen this, millions have heard it.' The reasoning was that of moral superiority and the acceptance of Indian rulers was an integral part of the experience of the Indian people, a part of their oral tradition. The British had to be defeated because their rule was based on deceit and was therefore morally reprehensible. The Indian people had accepted Indian rulers: the proof of this was in their undying loyalty to the line of Wajid Ali Shah. People were willing to die for this loyalty. The Begum's proclamation went beyond extolling this loyalty; it urged the rebels to continue to fight and not be distracted by the false promises of the British. There was work to be done and battles to be won.

At yet another level, the proclamation laid out the reasons for the rebellion. The war had to go on because it was about what was most important to people: their religion. It drove home the point that the rebellion began with religion and was fuelled by it. There was the deep-rooted fear and suspicion that the British rulers, through their deliberate policies, were trying to despoil the *deen* and the dharma of the common people of India. The proclamation, even at the end of 1858, played on this great fear to warn citizens of the real intentions of the British rulers and incited them in the name of religion to resist the British. By emphasizing this anxiety, the proclamation harked back to the summer of 1857 when the uprising had first begun. At that time, the fear had travelled by word of mouth, through rumours.

The first and the most alarming rumour for the sepoys was that the cartridges[5] had been greased with the fat of cows and pigs. Sepoys refused to take these cartridges and when they were punished for it, they mutinied. Witness what happened in Meerut on 10 May 1857. But almost immediately, the suspicion that caste and religion were in danger acquired much larger dimensions. From the cartridge, the fear of pollution extended to other items of daily use. One officer reported:

> Government, it was said, had sent up cartloads and boatloads of bone-dust, which was to be mixed up with the flour and sweetmeats sold in the bazaar, whereby the whole population would lose their caste. The public mind was greatly excited. On one day at Sultanpore it was spread over the station that a boat had arrived at a certain ghaut on the river Goomtee laden with bone-dust, and the sepoys were hardly restrained from outbreak. A few days later at the station of Salon, two camels laden with ammunition arrived at the house of Captain Thompson, the commandant. It was rumoured that the packages contained bone-dust and a panic spread through the station. Not only the sepoys in their lines, but the domestic servants about the officers' bungalows, and the villagers and zemindars attending court, hastily flung away, untasted the food which they had cooked, and fasted for the day. At Lucknow, the rumours which were whispered about were perpetual, and the public mind was never allowed to rest. Now it was at one shop, the next day in another bazaar, that despatches

of bone-dust had, it was asserted, been received. It was in vain that facts were opposed to the prevailing panic.[6]

In Sitapur, a day before the mutiny, the sepoys refused to touch the *atta* procured for them because they '. . . imagined it was adulterated and declared it would destroy their caste if they made use of it. This idea seemed to pervade the whole regiment, who declined to use the flour, notwithstanding the remonstrance of the commanding officer, whose efforts to convince them of the purity of the atta were entirely unavailing, and the men insisted on the whole being thrown into the river.'[7]

Salt, sugar, wheat, ghee and even water, it was believed, had been contaminated by a conspiracy hatched by the British, aimed at converting Hindus and Muslims to Christianity. The plot targeted all classes. The rumour said that the British had ordered all the princes, nobles, landholders, merchants and cultivators of the land 'to feed together upon English bread.'[8] That there was a conspiracy to convert Hindus and Muslims was a widely and firmly held belief. Henry Lawrence, the chief commissioner of Awadh, was 'startled by the dogged persistence' of a *jemadar* in the Awadh artillery—a man of 'excellent character', according to Lawrence, 'in the belief that for ten years past Government had been engaged in measures for the forcible or rather fraudulent conversion of all natives.'[9] Rumours about pollution and conversion spread panic. Untraceable in their origin and unverifiable in their import, they were pulled in a powerful current and touched on issues closest to Indian sentiments.

In the popular mind these rumours came to be linked with a prophecy floating around in 1857 that British rule would end at the centenary of Plassey.[10] Sitaram, a loyal sepoy, who left behind a rare account of his life in the British army, wrote, 'Our learned men . . . told us that the Company's rule would come to an end in 1857, since this was one hundred years after the Company's first great battle.'[11] The nature of this prediction and the way it was remembered rendered to it the character of what Keith Thomas called 'ancient prophecies' in the context of English popular culture of the sixteenth and seventeenth centuries. Such prophecies, Thomas noted, were invariably attributed to some mythical or historical personage ('our learned men', Sitaram wrote) and were always very old.[12] Kaye recorded an instance in which the prophecy about the end of British rule in 1857 had been made a thousand years earlier.[13] It circulated by word of mouth and acquired the character of a rumour.

Rumours, Ranajit Guha has pointed out in his study of peasant insurgency, were 'the *universal* and *necessary* carrier of insurgency in any pre-industrial and pre-literate society.'[14] Rumours, by definition authorless and spreading by word of mouth, became the transmitters of panic in 1857. Guha noted that because the transmission was oral, a socializing aspect was embedded in them. They were discussed where people assembled in large numbers.[15] Kaye noted this when he pejoratively described the rumours in the summer of 1857 as 'the lies of the bazaar.'[16] Because they were communicated orally, the rumours moved with remarkable speed from one station to another: Kaye wrote that the swiftness of the transmission was 'almost electric'. He picked up the Hindi saying, 'It is in the air', and added, 'We cannot trace the progress of these evil tidings . . . It often happened that an uneasy feeling . . . an impression that something had happened, though they could not discern the shape thereof—pervaded men's minds, in obscure anticipation of the news travelling towards them in all its tangible proportions.'[17] A rumour cannot be pinned down and this is what makes it, in Guha's words, 'a mobile and explosive agent of insurgency.' [18]

Rumours were not the only things circulating in north India in the summer of 1857. Chapatis miraculously started travelling too, and they became the most-talked about sensation of that year since they were first noticed in February–March 1857. The officer who was among the first to report the phenomenon left behind a vivid account: '. . . A signal has passed through numbers of the villages of this district, the purport of which has not yet transpired. The Chowkeydars of the villages bordering on those of Mutra have received small baked cakes of atta with orders to distribute them generally through the district. A Chowkeydar, upon receiving one of these cakes, has had five or six more prepared, and thus they have passed from village to village; so quickly has the order been executed that village after village has been served with this notice.'[19]

Another report from around the same time in the Agra division emerged with similar details:

In the commencement of 1857, while marching through Mynpoory district, my attention was drawn by Zemindars in villages adjoining the road to a mysterious distribution of chupatteess (or small wheaten cakes), with astonishing rapidity through the country. The bearers apparently knew no more than those from whom they last received the cakes what the purport of the injunction was which directed the preparation of the five cakes to be carried on to the villages in advance. 'They would be called for' it was stated, and in this way chupattees or their counterparts travelled often over 160 or 200 miles in a night . . . All endeavours failed to discover any explanation of this mysterious movement, [but] I have reason to believe that it had some bearing upon the Hindu prophecy limiting British rule to a centenary of years.[20]

It is significant that as soon as the movement of chapatis was first noticed, it was read as a signal for some unknown event. In the second instance, it was linked to the prophecy about the end of British rule a hundred years after Plassey. In the post-mortem of the uprising, British officers admitted that even though they were unsure about what the appearance of chapatis meant, they were certain that they were, in some way, linked to the uprising. This reading was summed up by one officer thus: 'The natives generally may have viewed this sign-manual flying through the villages . . . as a forerunner of some universal popular outbreak.'[21] Another officer saw the mystery of the chapatis solved by the outbreak of the revolt: 'I truly believe that the rural population of all classes, among whom these cakes spread, were as ignorant as I was myself of their real object; but it was clear they were a secret sign to be on the alert, and the minds of the people were through them kept watchful and excited. As soon as the disturbances broke out at Meerut and Delhi, the cakes explained themselves, and the people at once perceived what was expected of them.'[22] However, such an interpretation was not accepted by all British officers. R.H.W. Dunlop, a magistrate who had observed chapatis going round in his district, thought the attempts to link the chapatis to the uprising were 'without sufficient grounds'. He added that 'if any connection existed it was accidental and the relationship acknowledged by other designing or ignorant persons was consequent upon the distribution and did not cause or precede it.'[23] Indian nationalist historiography tended to dismiss any link between the revolt and the circulation of chapatis.[24]

Ranajit Guha added a completely new dimension to this bewildering phenomenon. He showed, by way of William Crooke's observations of rural life in northern India, that during an epidemic some ritually consecrated object was circulated to push the disease outside the boundaries of a village or a locality or a region. This operation was called *chalawa*, which means, according to Crooke, 'passing on the malady'. North India, just before 1857, had suffered a cholera epidemic and the chapati could have been the chalawa. A variant of this belief was already around in the aftermath of the uprising. E.A. Reade, the acting Lieutenant-Governor of the north-western provinces, thought that the connection of the chapatis with the rebellion arose out of a misunderstanding of a ritual—chalawa—on the part of J.R. Colvin, the Lieutenant-Governor of NWP, and had created an atmosphere of panic, raising the bogey of sedition. Standing apart from these interpretations, Guha wrote, 'The symbolic agent of an epidemic in the countryside it (the chapati) took on an added meaning as the carrier of an imminent but undefined political holocaust. No index of any kind of conspiracy, it connected neither with the past nor with the present. As an omen it looked ahead of events, and in an atmosphere charged with growing unrest in agrarian communities and army barracks it transmitted the rebellion in anticipation by sounding a tocsin for all to hear but none yet to understand why.'[25]

To return to the Begum's proclamation: this digression on rumours, chapatis and prophecies was necessary to emphasize two vital aspects of the rebellion which were important to appreciate the proclamation. One is the level and the speed of communication that existed at that time. Any information could be transmitted across large areas very fast. Thus, it is not at all surprising to read that the Begum's proclamation was 'extensively circulated, not only through the distant provinces of Oudh' and travelled as far as Delhi. The second is to highlight the role that religion played in the uprising—as springboard and mobilizer. The rumours and prophecies all centred on religion, seen not only as a series of ritual practices among Hindus and Muslims but also in the more profound sense conveyed in the notion of deen and dharma. The two terms are used to denote what holds a society together—modes of behaviour, a system of ethics and duties and morality. British rule, by its intrusions into the lives of Indians through various conquests and policies—political, economic and social—challenged the existing social and moral order in India. Threatened groups of Indians responded by trying to overthrow the British, who were considered agents of pollution. In this charged atmosphere, rumours, prophecies and ritually consecrated objects like chapatis spread in a virulent manner. How charged the atmosphere actually was and how deep-seated the suspicion of the plot to convert people to Christianity is illustrated by the fact that in Sitapur the very name of the Commissioner—Mr Christian—came to be identified with the religion and incited the wrath and fury of the rebels.[26] Another proclamation issued under the seal of Birjis Qadr but issued probably sometime in the first half of 1858 informed people that the 'British wish[ed] to deprive the Hindoos and Mahomedans of their religion and wish[ed] them to become Christians.'[27] People read these signs and announcements as they pleased—sources of panic or hope, or signals of imminent disaster. These were the springboards of rebel action. The Begum's proclamation returned to these issues as a last rallying cry. The rebellion began in the name of religion, and religion was what had motivated the common people to resist.

A group of sepoys, retreating into Nepal, put on record why they had fought:

> For a century ago the British arrived in Hindoostan and gradually entertained troops in their service, and became masters of every state. Our forefathers have always served them and we also entered their service. And we, as well as our children have received every kind of support from the govt. of the Company and we also were ready to serve them and wish them well. By the mercy of God, and with our assistance the British also conquered every place they liked, in which thousands of us, Hindoostani men were sacrificed, but we never made any excuses or pretences, nor revolted . . . But in the year 1857 the British issued an order that new cartridges and muskets which had arrived from England were to be issued; in the former of which the fats of cows and pigs were mixed; and also that attah of wheat mixed with powdered human bones was to be eaten; and even distributed them in every Regiment of infantry, cavalry and artillery. In Meerut there were the 11th Regiment N.I., the 20th Regiment N.I., 3rd Light Cavalry. They gave these

new cartridges to the sowars of the 3rd Light Cavalry, and ordered them to bite them; the troopers objected to it, and said that they would never bite, for if they did, their religion and faith would be destroyed. There have been many kings in Hindoostan but none have taken our religion and faith. The British also have been in India about a century, but they have never before acted in this manner. Upon this the British officers paraded the men of the 3 Regiments and having prepared 1400 English soldiers, and other Battalions of European troops and Horse Artillery, surrounded them, and placing 6 guns before each of the infantry regiments, loaded the guns with grape and made 84 new troopers prisoners, and put them in jail with irons on them. On this, we thought if we also objected, our lives and faith would be destroyed for nothing—for which reason we fought with the British and went to Delhie . . . The British say that we have only revolted for treasure and country, and by such deceptions have prevailed on those Rajahs and Chiefs to give them aid who do not pay a single thought to faith or religion . . . we have been compelled to make war for two years and the Rajahs and Chiefs who are with us in faith and religion, are still so, and have undergone all sorts of trouble; we have fought for two years in order that our faith and religion may not be polluted. If the religion of a Hindoo or Mussalman is lost, what remains in the world?[28]

A party of prisoners was individually asked before execution their reasons for the battle and war. Each one of them replied: 'The slaughter of the English was required by our religion.'[29] Religion was at the heart of the uprising and the Begum's proclamation recognized this.

Feroze Shah, a prince from Delhi, who fought briefly with the rebels in Awadh, issued a proclamation that repeated the charge that 'Within the last few years the British . . . under different pleas . . . continued to eradicate Hindoosim and Mahomedanism and to make all the people embrace Christianity.'[30] In this ishtahar, he circulated a list of the 'real intentions' of the British. Among these were (i) burning all the books of every other religion; (ii)making eating and drinking with Europeans compulsory for Indians seeking employment; (iii) destroying mosques and temples; (iv) forbidding Maulavis and Brahmins to preach; (v) administering all law courts according to English law; (vi) compelling all marriages to take place according to English customs under the supervision of English priests; (vii) prohibiting all prescriptions made out by Hindu and Muslim physicians, and substituting them with English medicine; (viii) disallowing Hindu and Muslim fakirs from converting people without the permission of Christian missionaries; (ix) allowing only European doctors to assist Indian women at childbirth. It is worth noting here that Shah saw himself as a herald of divinity. In the proclamation he wrote in messianic zeal: 'Placing my trust in God; devoting myself solely to God's service; observing the precepts of religion; strengthening my determination . . . my sword taken in my hand, the sword of religious zeal, I arise in the name of God. We shall obtain victory through the grace of God, who promises victory to those who put their trust in him. Therefore again I urge you, and urge you one and all, join me prompted solely by the desire of doing God's work.'[31]

Another proclamation, the date of which is difficult to specify, linked the war of words to the war of religion.[32] This one also carried the seal of Birjis Qadr and it had, unlike other ishtahars, a small prefatory note. This note said that the proclamation was to be circulated among the Hindus and Muslims of Hindustan. It added that the readers and the hearers should 'deeply reflect upon its contents and that all the Hindoos and Mahomedans whether women or men, may be ready to destroy the English for the purpose of defending their respective religions.' If they did not destroy the English, the faith of neither the Hindus nor the Muslims would remain, 'nor will his life nor his property, nor his children nor his honour be safe.' The destruction of the English was necessary because they threatened everything that was precious and cherished by Indians. But the most significant aspect of this note is the call that issues forth to the women of both communities. This is quite unique given the social conditions and the restrictions on women that prevailed in the 1850s among both Hindus and Muslims. This note and the proclamation made it the responsibility of women to join the fight to destroy the English. The destruction and defeat of the English was everyone's duty, regardless of faith and gender. Women were asked to transgress the restrictions imposed on them by tradition and custom and to defy the dominance of their fathers, husbands, brothers and so on. The defence of the faith was given greater importance than the tradition of male dominance. This appeal that everyone—both men and women—should fight highlights how serious the leadership was about tackling the threat of the English. In this context, it is no surprise that Hazrat Mahal and Lakshmibai put their lives at stake. There may have been others whose courage and actions have been forgotten.

This ishtahar adopted a line of attack that was somewhat unique. Even before the cartridge controversy, it said, the 'accursed English' had written to the 'Impure Victoria' seeking permission to kill fifteen maulavis and fifteen priests out of every hundred respectively. In addition, if they could kill 500,000 'Hindoo and Mahomedan sepoys and Ryuts,' they would 'in a short time make all the people of India "Christians".' According to the proclamation, the British wanted a genocide in India to make way for their conversion project. The ishtahar continued: 'Then that ill-starred polluted Bitch gave her consent to the spilling of innocent blood. She did not reflect at all that she was not at liberty to permit the commission of the murder of the creatures of God.' Having got her consent, the 'accursed men commenced committing general slaughter on the pretext of the cartridges.' The proclamation claimed that since there was no opposition at the time, everyone who refused to become a Christian would have been killed in a short time but 'by God's blessings, the bold sepoys butchered the English and put an end to all their power.' The sepoys had rendered the English so weak that 'it [had] been easy to kill or expel them.' It urged the people to 'be engaged in taking steps for their [the British] destruction' and appealed that none of the Hindus and Muslims serve them in any way. The ishtahar then acquired a sharper moral tenor: 'It has become the bounden duty of all the people, whether women or men, slave girls or slaves, to come forward and put the English to death.' The mention of slave girls is significant since Hazrat Mahal was the daughter of a slave.

The proclamation proceeded to describe how this destruction could be achieved. The religious leaders—maulavis and pundits—should go around every village and city explaining the misfortunes that would befall people if the British were successful, and conversely highlighting the advantages and 'spiritual benefit' to them if the British were to be destroyed. Further, 'the Kings, Wuzeers, Rajahs and Nawabs ought to slay them in the field of battle'. The people should not leave their city when the British entered it—this suggests that the ishtahar was issued when Colin Campbell and his army entered Lucknow, either in November 1857 or March 1858. There followed a series of instructions regarding how to fight the British once they had entered the city: '[the people] should shut up their doors and all the people whether men, women or children, including slave girls, slaves and old women, ought to put these accursed English to death by firing guns, carbines and pistols from the terraces, shooting arrows and pelting them with stones, bricks, earthen vessels, ladles, old shoes and all other things which may come into their hands.' The attack on the British should be united and unrestrained. It is worth recalling that when the British troops entered Lucknow first under Outram and Havelock and then under Campbell, they did meet, as seen in the previous chapter, this kind of resistance.

The no-holds barred approach was elaborated in more graphic terms:

The sepoys, the nobles, the shopkeepers, the oil men, etc. and all other people of the city, being of one accord, should make a simultaneous attack upon them, some of them should kill them by firing guns, pistols, and carbines and with swords, arrows, daggers, poignando, etc., some lift them up on spears, some dexterously snatch their arms and destroy the enemy, some should cling to their necks, some to their waists, some should wrestle and through stratagem break the enemy to pieces; some should strike them with cudgels, some slap them, some throw dust in their eyes, some should beat them with shoes, some attack them with their fists, some scratch them, some drag them along, some tear out their ears, some break their noses. In short no one should spare any efforts, to destroy the enemy and reduce them to the greatest extremities.

Such a people's resistance would guarantee that the British would 'be unable to do anything, though they may amount to lakhs of men.' Everybody should fight the British and this would ensure their defeat. It was everyone's war because the war was about religion. To make certain that this happened, 'It was necessary to make this Proclamation generally known.'

The proclamation discussed above was circulated with a pamphlet called 'Fateh-i Islam'.[33] The pamphlet is not dated but the editors of the *Freedom Struggle in Uttar Pradesh* volumes suggest a date based on the internal evidence of the text. Their logic is as follows: The first four paragraphs of the pamphlet speak about the atrocities committed by the British and attempt to rally the people to wage a holy war against them. The pamphlet invokes the efforts made by the sepoys and the common people to attack the entrenchment in Kanpur and in the battles in Delhi and Lucknow. It refers to the atrocities committed in Allahabad, which took place after 18 June 1857. There is also a call to defend Delhi and Kanpur. This would suggest that the document was prepared sometime between 5 July and 17 July 1857—in other words, between the coronation of Birjis Qadr that followed the rebel victory at Chinhat (30 June 1857) and the fall of Kanpur. The latter event made it evident that the next port of call for the British counter-insurgency forces would be Lucknow.

This was also the period when Maulavi Ahmadullah Shah was very active in Lucknow.[34] Did he have a hand in drafting the pamphlet?

The authorship of the document is much less important than what it has to say, especially because it was the longest statement to emerge from the rebel side. 'Fateh-i Islam' began with an invocation to the prophet Mohammed but moved very quickly to the oppression of the British. It is significant that the British were referred to by their religion: 'The execrable Christians are openly committing oppression and tyranny; they are killing innocent men, plundering their property, setting fire to their houses and shutting up their children in houses, some of which they burn down . . . Such has been the state of anarchy, that the whole country has been insecure and plunderers are robbing the villagers and travellers . . . They [the British] are also hanging men and ravaging villages.' Going by this list of atrocities and what soon followed, it is clear that the actions of the troops under James Neill as they marched from Allahabad to Kanpur are being spoken of.[35]

The pamphlet lamented that there had been a delay in fighting the Christians, but this only made the cause of religious war more urgent. If the Christians were not defeated, 'great misfortunes {would] befall all the Hindoos and Mahomedans, the people, the sepoys, the Kings and the Wuzeers.' Fortunately, the cause of a religious war had been furthered by the possession of guns, 'which the people of Hindoostan stood in need of'. These guns were previously with the 'Mahomedan Kings of Delhi and Lucknow'. Now they seemed to be more widely available to all those engaged in the war against the Christians. The moment was opportune to defeat the Christians.

The pamphlet then moved on to a different trajectory altogether. It asserted that 'formerly it was not in the power of even the Nawabs and the Rajas to kill even a common sepoy of the British, but now shoemakers and sellers of spirituous liquors have destroyed British gentlemen.' The suggestion was that the world had been turned upside down and that the British were no longer considered as superiors. They were being attacked and killed by common people. The perpetrators were now the victims. The pamphlet incited the sepoys to kill the Christians and assured them that they would not be held responsible on Judgment Day. It went on to allege that the Christians were using various forms of enchantment to deceive the sepoys, but that the latter could protect themselves from such magic 'by the repetition of the invocation Allah-Akber.' The primary duty of the sepoys was the 'protection of Delhi and Lucknow . . . as these two places [were] the asylums of the sepoys and the people high and low.' It urged the sepoys to proceed as far as Calcutta, after having securing those two cities. Significantly, the pamphlet strictly forbade plunder: 'The enemies have plundered those for whose protection you are going. If you also plunder them, to whom will you look for protection? Punish immediately the plunderer and cause the plundered property to be restored to its owner. Pillage is the part of a criminal . . . It is however lawful to plunder the property of the enemy; such plundered property is designated "Prize".' The pamphlet went on note: Both common sense and regard for faith 'point out that servitude under the Mahomedan Chiefs and such Rajahs as are dependents of the Mahomedan Kings is infinitely better than that, under the infidel Victoria and the English, the enemies of our faith.'

For a pamphlet titled 'Fateh-i Islam', the most remarkable feature of its contents is what it had to say to the Hindus.

> 'The Hindoos,' the pamphlet wrote, 'should join the Chief with a view to defend their religion, and should solemnly pledge themselves (to be faithful); the Hindoos and the Mahomedans, as brethren to each other, should also butcher the English, inasmuch as formerly the Mahomedan Kings protected (as they felt it incumbent on them to do so) the lives and property of the Hindoos with their children in the same manner as they protected those of the Mahomedans, and all the Hindoos with heart and soul were obedient and loyal to the Mahomedan Kings . . . The Hindoos will remain steadfast to their religion, while we will also retain ours. Aid and protection will be offered by us to each other.

This was a clear statement that the fight against the British was not confined to any one section of the people. The British had targeted all Indians, irrespective of their religion, and the pamphlet made out that it was the moral duty of all Hindus and Muslims to annihilate the British.

This introduces a major theme of the ishtahars, without exception. All of them appealed to Hindus and Muslims and emphasized the necessity of unitedly fighting the British. What was invariably invoked, as in 'Fateh-i Islam', was the pre-British Hindu–Muslim coexistence—'as brethren to each other'—within the Mughal imperial framework. The proclamation issued in the name of Bahadur Shah on 25 August 1857—often called the Azamgarh Proclamation—declared:

I, who am the grandson of Abul Muzuffer Serauddin Bahadur Shah Ghazee, King of India, having in the course of circuit come here to extirpate the infidels . . . and to liberate and protect the poor helpless people now groaning under their iron rule, have, by the aid of the Majahdeens . . . erected the standard of Mahommed, and persuaded the orthodox Hindoos who had been subject to my ancestors, and have been and are still accessories in the destruction of the English, to raise the standard of Mahavir.[36]

The idea of a united fight against the British was enacted on the ground as witnessed by the British failure to raise the Hindu population of Bareilly against Muslims in 1857. One British officer recorded, '. . . [the Chief Commissioner] had authorized the sum of Rs 50,000 to be expended in an attempt to raise the Hindoo population of Bareilly against the Maohmmedan rebels . . . the attempt was quite unsuccessful and has been abandoned.'[37] The most telling and poignant instance of this unity was the hailing of Birjis Qadr by the rebel sepoys as 'our Kanahiya.'

A critical aspect of maintaining the rebel forces was payment to the troops. In the initial stages of the rebellion, it was reported that the old sepoys of the Awadh army received Rs 12 a month, and the regiments that had come from Delhi received Rs 7.[38] The rebel leadership in Awadh compensated the families of sepoys who were killed in action with a sum of Rs 100; those sepoys who were wounded received Rs 50.[39] As late as September 1858, this promise was reiterated: 'Every sepoy should know that the heirs of those who fall will be maintained by the Sirkar and those who are wounded will get compensations for their wounds.'[40] As the rebellion entered its later and desperate stage and faced imminent defeat and suppression, maintaining these rates became impossible. In July 1858, the cavalry and the infantry under Khan Bahadur Khan were receiving only four annas and one anna respectively per day.[41] In the Begum's camp at Baundi around September 1858, the sepoys received one anna eight pi per day; and at Bala Rao's camp near Bahraich, the troops were being paid two annas per day.[42] The strain was severe. Rana Beni Madho, a leading rebel taluqdar who was with Hazrat Mahal in the course of the flight to Nepal, sent a petition in July 1858 in which he wrote, 'The conditions obtaining here [southern Awadh] are not very encouraging. The troops stationed at Salon demand their arrears of pay from the Chakledar, Muhammad Fazl Azim Khan Bahadur and the Taluqdars, who make professions of loyalty, harbour designs of the non-payment of half of the government dues as allowed to them by the Sarkar. Under such conditions it is not possible to pay the daily allowance to the troops, as sanctioned by the Government.'[43]

The rebel leadership was fully aware of its duties and obligations to the people. The Azamgarh Proclamation, for example, set down in precise terms the grievances of the different sections of the population—the rich, zamindars, merchants, public servants, sepoys, artisans, pundits, fakirs and other learned persons—and appealed to them to join the war against the firangi. But there was an affiliation with the interests of the landed magnates and the propertied classes. The ishtahar said, '. . . in the Badshahi Government . . . the Jumas will be light, the dignity and honour of the zemindars safe, and every zemindar will have absolute rule in his own zemindary.' A proclamation of Birjis Qadr observed that in pre-British times, property being 'dear to every man' was never confiscated, whereas under the British, property was not sacrosanct. The same proclamation added that all pre-British sarkars had preserved the izzat of the people and had allowed every man 'to possess his honour according to his worth and capacity, be he a person of good descent, of any caste or community, Syud, Sheikh, Moghul or Pathan, among the Mahomedans or Brahmin, Chhuttree, Bais or Kaith among the Hindoos. All these retain their respectability according to their respective ranks, and no person of a lower order such as sweeper, chamar, Dhanook or Pasee can claim equality with them.' But under the *angrez sarkar*, the same proclamation stated: 'The honour and respectability of the higher orders are considered by them equal to the honour and respectability of the lower orders, nay, comparatively with the latter they treat the former, with contempt and disrespect; and at the instance of a chamar force the attendance of a Nawab or a Rajah and subject him to indignity.'[44] The uprising was expressly not aspiring to establish an egalitarian society. It was harking back to a pattern of society where hierarchy and deference mattered, where some ruled and some obeyed, where the patronage extended by the superiors was bound by a sense of honour and obligation. This society had existed since time immemorial in India; it was different from a society based on merit and contract that the British were trying to inflict on the Indian people. It was this imposition of an alien order that had to be resisted by all. This espousal of property, hierarchy and honour was in complete conformity with the world that Mughal rule had represented. It was this world that the rebel leadership recalled in their ishtahars. In their war with words, the rebel leaders invoked the world as it had once been—under the Mughals and other pre-British political dispensations. British rule had sought to destroy this familiar world and the values embodied in it. The indignation that was at the core of the ishtahars aimed to restore the old world that the British were bent on overthrowing. Rebel leadership was not without aims and aspirations. It was imbued with a certain kind of consciousness.

*

Lakshmibai has been conspicuous by her absence in the above discussion, which has concentrated on issues that were raised in the ishtahars circulated in the names of Hazrat Mahal, Birjis Qadr, Bahadur Shah and other leaders located in the heart of the Gangetic plain. These ishtahars were also suggestive of a style of leadership and the aims and aspirations of the uprising. Lakshmibai's theatre of activities was Jhansi, in a remote part of what was then the North-Western Provinces. The circumstances in which she found herself provided her neither the time nor the opportunity to participate in what I have called the war of words. Her activities were more rooted in arms and located in the actual battlefield. As has been noted in the previous chapter, once the sepoys in Jhansi had mutinied and killed the firangi they sped away to Delhi. Lakshmibai was left to organize affairs in Jhansi. Her first task was to protect what she considered her territory and her inheritance from the chiefs and rajas who wanted to invade and claim Jhansi. The British recognized her as the *pro tem* ruler of Jhansi given the crisis of authority. She wrote to the British to plead that she was doing her best to administer and maintain order and that the British should provide succour as soon as possible. No help was forthcoming to her from any quarter, and it became clear that she would have to fend for herself on two fronts: against the rebels, who suspected her of dragging her feet in joining the rebellion, and against the British, who were convinced, without a shred of evidence, that she was responsible for the massacre of the Europeans in Jhansi and thus had to be eliminated in an act of vengeance. As Hugh Rose's army encircled Jhansi, Lakshmibai was left with no other alternative but to go forth into battle to protect and preserve her honour. She therefore had little or no time to engage in a war of words. She entered the war of arms somewhat belatedly and reluctantly, but it was in that war that she left her indelible mark.

Without in any way gainsaying the above, there are a few loose ends regarding Lakshmibai that need to be dealt with. Immediately after the mutiny, as noted earlier, the sepoys issued a proclamation that declared, 'The people are God's, the country is the king's, and the two religions govern.'[45] This was the first public rebel utterance in Jhansi. It is significant that the sepoys invoked the Badshah and not the ruler of Jhansi. Once the sepoys left, Lakshmibai issued a second proclamation in which she announced: the 'raj is Lachmee Bai's.'[46] Lakshmibai was thus publicly staking her claims on Jhansi. It is possible to detect here a divergence between the aims of the sepoys and the aspirations of Lakshmibai. Did this divergence influence the rebels' feelings of suspicion towards Lakshmibai in the later stages of the uprising? The question cannot completely be set aside.

Sen, in his book on 1857, deals with a letter that Lakshmibai allegedly wrote in Hindi to her family priest in

Puri. It would appear from this letter, dated March 1856, that Lakshmibai was engaged in organizing an uprising against the British more than one year before the sepoys and the people of Meerut raised the flag of rebellion. Sen points out a number of discrepancies in this letter. Firstly, both the language and the script were not those that were prevalent in the middle of the nineteenth century. Secondly, the letters from Lakshmibai that survived, especially those that she wrote to Robert Hamilton (referred to earlier in this book), followed the Muslim style of dating and the Islamic calendar. But this letter to the priest followed the English mode of dating and the English calendar. Thirdly, the seal used in this letter sent to Puri was different from the one that was used in the letters to Hamilton. Last, but certainly not the least, this letter referred to the greased cartridges. The cartridges of the Enfield Rifle did not come to India before November 1856 and the sepoys did not have any information about them till January 1857. This letter by Lakshmibai was purportedly written from Meerut. There is no evidence that she was in Meerut in March 1856 or at any other time. The letter, Sen correctly concludes, was 'a clumsy fabrication.'[47]

There was a letter or a proclamation[48] going around in Jhansi in late 1857 that enumerated the violations that the British had carried out as 'perverters of all men's religion'. In the list were included activities of missionaries and legal measures such as widow remarriage and abolition of sati. Further, the British had prohibited adopted sons from inheriting kingdoms, and this was seen as 'the stratagems by which the Europeans deprive us of our thrones and wealth, for instance I refer to Nagpore and Lucknow.' The document went on to urge the Hindus in the name of Ganga, Tulsi and Salikram, and Muslims in the name of God to 'join us, destroying the English for their mutual welfare. Let not this opportunity pass away. Know Oh the people! You will never have such another.' This letter was picked up in the bazaars of Jhansi, and Hamilton, when he forwarded Lakshmibai's letter to him to Calcutta, included this document. The British saw this as an appeal made by Lakshmibai. In reality, this had been printed by Maulavi Syed Kutab Shah at the Bahaduri Press in Bareilly and Lakshmibai had nothing to do with it.[49]

Lakshmibai had thus not been a participant in the war of words in 1857–58. She entered the stage of history without a script but in the most dramatic way.

AFTERLIFE

When, on the night of 4 April 1858, Lakshmibai escaped on horseback from the fort in Jhansi, she rode into history. And when, on 17 June, she died fighting in Kota ki-Serai, she became a legend. It is assumed that the British in their thirst for vengeance demonized her. This, however, is not entirely true. When the British encountered her in battle, their assessment of her was very different. Hugh Rose in his official despatch on the taking of Kalpi observed: 'The high descent of the Ranee, her unbounded liberality to her Troops and retainers, and her fortitude which no reverses could shake, rendered her an influential and dangerous adversary.'[1] This sentence is revelatory about both Lakshmibai and the attitude of the British towards her. They admired her courage in the face of adversity. She was a force to reckon with, and therefore she was a formidable enemy. The influence she commanded was based on the way she treated and looked after her troops and retainers. Their loyalty towards her was grounded in her patronage and generosity. There was, however, another source of her influence that Rose drew attention to in the very first five words of his statement, where he spoke about Lakshmibai's pedigree—'high descent'. By this Rose was not referring to her parental provenance, which was not aristocratic. He was obviously referring to the fact that she was a queen, a rani. As a rani, Lakshmibai commanded the loyalty of her people because as a rani she deemed it her responsibility to look after them. The British may have dethroned the dynasty into which Lakshmibai had married, but they could not ignore the loyalty she enjoyed, because the raj in Jhansi was indeed Lakshmibai's.

The love and faithfulness of the people towards Lakshmibai were expressed in many folk songs that began to do the rounds in and around Jhansi within a few years after her death. Folk memory immortalized Lakshmibai by making her into a legend. During the 1857 centenary, P.C. Joshi, leader and quondam General Secretary of the Communist Party of India, tramped around Jhansi to collect these songs.[2] They show how she was revered and eventually immortalized. One song, whose refrain would become famous in a very popular twentieth-century poem by Subhadra Kumari Chauhan, eulogized Lakshmibai thus:

> How valiantly like a man fought she,
> the Rani of Jhansi!
> On every parapet a gun she set,
> Raining fire of hell,
> How well like a man fought the Rani of Jhansi,
> How valiantly and well!

The poem '*Khoob lari mardani, woh jo Jhansi wali Rani thi*' will be discussed later in this chapter.

According to folk memory, the chief gunner in Lakshmibai's artillery was one Ghulam Gaus Khan, whose friend Khudadad Khan guarded the main gate of the Jhansi fort. Both were killed while defending the fort. A song commemorated their deaths through Khudadad Khan's dying words:

> We have to die one day, brother
> and I shall choose today
> For our queen I shall lay down
> my life.
> I shall hack the Firanghi with my
> sword/ And the world will forever remember me.

Another song remembered that Lakshmibai's army was a people's army raised from among the common people:

> From clay and stones
> She moulded her army.
> From mere wood
> She made swords.
> And the mountain she transformed
> into a steed.
> Thus she marched to Gwalior.

One song recorded how Lakshmibai had ordered the felling of trees between Jalaun and Kalpi:

> Fell the trees,
> commanded the Rani of Jhansi
> Lest the Firanghis hang
> our soldiers on them

So that the coward British
may not be able to shout:
'Hang! Hang them in the trees!'
So that, in the hot sun
they may have no shade.

The reference here is obviously to the acts of vengeance that
the troops under Neill carried out as they marched down
the Grand Trunk Road from Allahabad to Kanpur. William
Howard Russell, the correspondent for *The Times*, recorded
that an officer who had been part of Neill's column told him,
'In two days forty-two men were hanged on the roadside, and
a batch of twelve men were executed because their faces were
'turned the wrong way' when they were met on the march.'[3]
Another report acknowledged 'the indiscriminate hanging
not only of persons of all shades of guilt but of those whose
guilt was at the least very doubtful . . . the innocent as well as
the guilty, without regard to age or sex, were indiscriminately
punished and in some cases sacrificed.'[4] P.C. Joshi pointed
out that by ordering the cutting of trees, Lakshmibai, as a
military strategist, was carrying out a 'scorched earth' policy.[5]
One might add that trees could also be obstacles to a free line
of fire. Lakshmibai may have been thinking of that, if indeed
she had given the orders to have the trees felled. There was
another angle that is suggested in the last two lines of the
song: 'So that, in the hot sun / they may have no shade.' It
is on record that Hugh Rose was alarmed by the heat and
the absence of water as his troops neared Kalpi. He observed
in his official despatch: 'They [the troops] had to encounter
also a new antagonist, a Bengal Sun, at its maximum heat . . .
Forage also was as scant as water . . . The scarcity of water

had another disadvantage; it prevented concentration of my Force, when the strength of the enemy, and my difficulties rendered it necessary for a rapid advance against Culpee.'[6] Lakshmibai's tactics, as described in the song, seemed to have paid dividends. The plight of the British was captured in another song:

> Amidst tears from his eyes
> Proud Hugh Rose spoke:
> I beg you for one pot of water
> To quench my thirst
> With the first potful
> and ask for more
> (To get that covered pot)
> Hand over the guns
> the ammunition
> And also your sword.

The imprint that Lakshmibai left on folk memory is in sharp contrast to the absence of any such recollection of Hazrat Mahal and her resistance to the British in the culture and traditions of the people of Awadh. The ICS officer William Crooke, who went around north India in the late nineteenth and early twentieth centuries collecting folk songs about the rebellion, Wajid Ali Shah, the imposition of British rule and so on did not record a single song about Hazrat Mahal and Birjis Qadr, with the exception of a passing mention of them in a verse of a long song.[7] Crooke called the song 'The Settlement of Oudh' and the relevant verse goes like this:

What kind of bravery did Birjis Qadr, the Queen show?
Her name has remained in the world.
Who will ever show such courage?
When the Queen had fled what fight was possible?[8]

Other than this one verse the resistance left no visible mark on folk memory. Ironically, the second line of the verse predicted 'Her name has remained in the world.' But it hasn't. The reason for this strange forgetting is perhaps suggested in the last line of the verse: 'When the Queen had fled what fight was possible?' Hazrat Mahal had given up the battle to protect her life, and her escape made any resistance meaningless. Hazrat Mahal had been a rebel from the beginning and had displayed, as the song records, unbelievable courage—a courage that would have made her name immortal. But in the end she became a fugitive—she fled, leaving her people with no choice other than to renounce the resistance. Lakshmibai, on the other hand, had been initially reluctant to join the rebellion but once she had joined the revolt, she did not flee; she died in battle like her people. Lakshmibai was thus eulogized in folk memory through songs; Hazrat Mahal's bravery was not forgotten but she was remembered, and her state lamented in the verse of a song. Death deifies; flight is an amnesiac.

*

The high praise that Hugh Rose bestowed on Lakshmibai's pedigree and her impact was echoed by Kaye in his history of what he dubbed the 'Sepoy War'. Kaye wrote, 'Evil things were said of her; for it is a custom among us—*odisse quem laeseris*—to take a Native ruler's kingdom and then to revile the deposed ruler or his would-be-successor. It was alleged that the Ranee was a mere child under the influence of others, and that she was much given to intemperance. That she was not a mere child was demonstrated by her conversation; and her intemperance seems to be a myth.'[9] The volume of Kaye's history that contained these observations was published in 1876. It would not be wrong to conclude from what Kaye wrote that in the immediate aftermath of the uprising, there were canards floating around about Lakshmibai. Kaye did not spell out the nature of her alleged intemperance: the word can be an indicator of many sins, from a volatile temper to a fondness for liquor to sexual promiscuity. Kaye dismissed the allegation in the softest possible terms—'seems to be a myth', not *is a myth*. It need hardly be emphasized that intemperance, in Victorian times, was a euphemism for promiscuity.

This depiction of Lakshmibai as an intemperate person— possibly in the sexual sense—can be traced back to the way her appearance was described by John Lang, the first white person to see her. Lang wrote:

> She was a woman of about middle size—rather stout but not too stout. Her face must have been very handsome when she was younger, and even now it had many charms— though according to my idea of beauty, it was too round. The expression was also very good, and very intelligent. The eyes were particularly fine, and the nose very delicately shaped. She was not very fair, though she was far from black. She had no ornaments, strange to say, upon her person, except for a pair of gold ear-rings. Her dress was a

110

plain white muslin, so fine in texture, and drawn about her in such a way, and so tightly, that the outline of her figure was plainly discernible—and a remarkably fine figure she had.[10]

The male gaze is stark in the passage. This, when combined with racial hatred, removed the veil of euphemism. Forrest, in 1912, described Lakshmibai as an 'ardent, daring, licentious woman'.[11] A rebel woman had to be shorn of all morality: she had to be reduced to a whore.

Sen pointed out that the adjectives that Forrest used were borrowed from the report of Macpherson, the political agent of Gwalior, written in 1858. Sen tried to justify those words by saying that his report was meant 'only for official eyes.' Forrest, according to Sen, ignored the observations of Malcolm that Lakshmibai had a very high character and was loved and respected by everyone in Jhansi. Forrest repeated the conviction shared by contemporary British officials that Lakshmibai was responsible for the massacre in Jhansi—an act, according to Forrest, 'as revolting and deliberate' as the massacre in Kanpur. Lakshmibai was guilty without evidence and this sanctioned the spread of any kind of calumny about her character. Vengeance, even more than fifty years after the event, triumphed over fact.

Given this bloodstain on Lakshmibai's hands, one of the first tasks that Indian historians took upon themselves was to absolve her of the murder of the white population in Jhansi. The Marathi writer-scholar D.B. Parasnis, who published in 1894 an account of Lakshmibai's life and career in Marathi—the first by any Indian—claimed that Lakshmibai's adopted son, Damodar Rao, had shown him a letter written to him by the British officer Martin, stating that Lakshmibai had been falsely charged and was, in fact, completely innocent. In that letter, dated 20 August 1889, Martin wrote:

> Your poor mother was very unjustly and cruelly dealt with—and no one knows her true case as I do. The poor thing took no part whatever in the massacre of the European residents of Jhansi in June 1857. On the contrary she supplied them with food for 2 days after they had gone into the Fort—got 100 match-lock men from Kurrura, and sent them to assist us, but after being kept a day in the Fort, they were sent away in the evening. She then advised Major Skene and Captain Gordon to fly at once to Dattia and place themselves under the Raja's protection, but this even they would not do; and finally they were all massacred by our own troops—the police, Jail & Cas: Este (sic).[12]

A question mark hangs over the provenance of this letter: in 1957, when Sen wrote his book, he noted in a footnote to the letter just quoted that 'Damodar Rao's son lives at Imli Bazar, Indore. Martin's letter cannot be traced, but Parasnis claims to have seen it.' How far could these claims be trusted? It needs to be noted that Parasnis did not depend solely on Martin's letter to Damodar Rao to establish Lakshmibai's innocence. In the words of Prachi Deshpande, 'Parasnis's trump card for establishing Lakshmibai's innocence in the massacre of Europeans was that no documentary proof pointed to her involvement.'[13]

To understand what Parasnis was trying to do in his biography—an extremely important text since it was the first in an emerging nationalist genre—it is necessary to locate it within the intellectual discourse prevalent in the closing decades of the nineteenth century—a discourse whose thrust was to challenge and overturn the dominance of the writings of British historians over India's past. It was a battle to control the past. The clarion call for this battle came from the pen of Bankimchandra Chattopadhyay, Bengali writer and intellectual, who wrote in 1880: 'Bengal must have her own history. Otherwise, there is no hope for Bengal. Who is to write it? You have to write it. I have to write it. All of us have to write it. Anyone who is a Bengali has to write it. Come, let us join our efforts in investigating the history of Bengal . . . It is not a task that can be done by any one person alone; it is a task for all of us to do together.'[14]

Though written by a Bengali for Bengalis, Ranajit Guha, quoting the passage, pointed out that Bengal and Bengali were notations for India and Indian, and for other regions of the sub-continent. According to Guha, what the statement was setting forth was an agenda—the responsibility for constructing an 'Indian historiography of India'. Indians had to represent themselves by claiming a past that was free from the distortions and slanders that foreign interpreters and historians had introduced. The very act of self-representation that was entailed in the writing of one's own history was nothing short of a political act since it challenged the assumption that the British could represent India's past and its present. There was another aspect of Chattopadhyay's declaration that did not receive adequate emphasis. This was the question of agency. Who was to write the Indian historiography of India? The people of India would write it— 'you, I, all of us'—in Bankimchandra's words. There was no need for any academic training. The Indian past was free and open to be claimed by any and every Indian.

It would be unrealistic to expect that Chattopadhyay's call, since it was uttered in Bengali, was heard across India. But people in other parts of the country, most certainly in Maharashtra, had similar ideas about reclaiming India's past. Individuals like N.J. Kirtane and K.N. Sane were pioneers in this project in Maharashtra. The former, while still a first-year student at Deccan College, Pune, had in 1868 published in Marathi a critique of Grant Duff's *History of the Marathas*, which had appeared in 1826. Sane, also from Pune, had started a periodical called *Kavyetihas Samgraha* (A Collection of Historical and Poetic Works). Parasnis belonged to this early band of amateur scholars and historians. In terms of formal education, he had not gone beyond high school and had published a short-lived magazine as an adolescent. As a young adult, he became an intermediary between government officials and princes. He had great personal charm and was well liked by the princes and the administrators. He used these connections not for personal benefit but to push forward his agenda for research on the history of the Marathas. The historian and archivist V.G. Khobrekar wrote of Parasnis, 'During the period of his visits to the [princely] courts and the [government] offices, Parasnis did not swerve from his cherished aim: that of collecting and printing old historical papers, of publishing old pictures and providing material for historical research.'[15]

It was this enthusiasm for reconstructing Maharashtra's history and the appropriation of the past for nation-building that led a twenty-something Parasnis to Lakshmibai. Sumit Guha captures this through the following anecdote. In 1890, during the Spring Festival in Pune, one Pandit Vasantrao delivered a public lecture on the subject 'The History of the Provinces of the Northwest and Ayodhya in the Past Thirty Years'. The lecture contained many stories about Lakshmibai and was reported in the Pune newspaper *Kesari* on 27 May 27 1890. Parasnis wrote, 'Pandit Vasantrao had narrated this widely known story in a spicy novelistic way. His delivery was also attractive and pleasing, and the listeners found it most enjoyable. Other inhabitants of Pune also enjoyed it through the newspaper *Kesari's* report. This revived interest in and appreciation of the Rani.' Parasnis added that his own biography of Lakshmibai, which he published in 1894, was an indirect outcome of this lecture and the report about it.

The biography had a more immediate and contentious context. Parasnis noted that people in Pune were oblivious of the existence of Lakshmibai's adopted son Damodar Rao, who was upset about the many false stories circulating about his mother. He wrote a letter to the *Kesari* (published on 10 June 1890) challenging the stories and asked to see what evidence Vasantrao had to back them. The *Kesari* published an apology and as Vasantrao had no evidence to offer, he too apologized. It was this—the spread of misleading accounts and the desire to know the truth about Lakshmibai—that motivated Parasnis to embark on a historical biography of Lakshmibai. Parasnis's first port of call was Rao, who gave him all the information he had—his own experiences and memories, as well as those of old retainers and surviving documents. Among these must have been the letter that Martin had written to him about Lakshmibai's innocence.

Parasnis thus began his project by comparing the documents he had received from Rao with the narratives of the uprising that British historians had produced after 1857. He found many contradictions, and spurred by them he travelled to Jhansi in search of sources. His biography, he claimed, was based on a study and scrutiny of all the sources that he had been able to obtain. Parasnis's project, as Sumit Guha suggests, is indicative of the emergence of a historical consciousness in Maharashtra.[16] That consciousness also had a radical salience to it—the removal of the stigma and slander that British historians and their followers had smeared on the figure of Lakshmibai. Parasnis's attempt was to write an Indian history of Lakshmibai and it was powered by the need to correct the misrepresentations she had been subjected to by British writers. The correction of the misrepresentations would be the first step towards establishing the truth and an assertion to represent one's own history. It was nothing short of a declaration of a national consciousness that was not yet fully aware of its own radical potential.

That power did not take long to manifest itself. It came in 1909, within two years of the fiftieth anniversary of the uprising, in Marathi, from the pen of a Marathi man, not yet thirty. V.D. Savarkar in 1907 was in London, enrolled to become a barrister-at-law at Gray's Inn. While growing up in various towns of Maharashtra he had already imbibed and advocated revolutionary ideas. He pursued these with even greater vigour in London. He wanted to be part of a movement that would successfully overthrow British rule in India.[17] His inspiration was the Italian revolutionary leader Mazzini, in whom his interest deepened as he read more about him while in London; he translated Mazzini's autobiography into Marathi.[18] Upon completion of this translation, Savarkar decided to write about the revolt of 1857 after he read Kaye's book on the subject. Savarkar began his research in the India Office in London.[19] From this exploration was born *The Indian War of Independence of 1857*—a book that has become a milestone in the literature on the uprising.[20]

The premises of the arguments of the book were presented during a commemoration of the revolt on its fiftieth anniversary. Under Savarkar's leadership the young men who lived at India House in London organized a function on 11 May 1907. The invitation read: 'Under the auspices of the Free India League it is decided to commemorate the golden jubilee of the patriotic rising of 1857. The meeting is to be held on Saturday 11th of May, the day of the declaration of Independence.' India House was specially decorated for the occasion. Savarkar delivered a rousing speech titled 'O! Martyrs!' In the words of his biographer, Savarkar said 1857 'was a rehearsal of sorts for a permanent war in India that would not rest till it witnessed a complete overthrow of the Empire.' He declaimed:

Today is the 10th of May! (sic). It was on this day that, in the ever-memorable year of 1857, the first campaign of the War of Independence was opened by you Oh Martyrs, on the battlefield of India . . . all honour be to you, Oh Martyrs; for it was for the preservation of the honour of the race that you performed the fiery ordeal of a revolution . . . this day . . . we dedicate, Oh Martyrs to your inspiring memory! It was on this day that you raised a new flag to be upheld, you uttered a mission to be fulfilled, you saw a mission to be realized . . . We take up your cry, we revere your flag, we are determined to continue that fiery mission of 'away with the foreigner', which you uttered, amidst the prophetic thundering of the Revolutionary war. Revolutionary, yes, it was a Revolutionary war . . . No, a revolutionary war knows no truce, save liberty or death! Indians these words must be fulfilled! Your blood, oh Martyrs, shall be avenged! . . . For the War of 1857 shall not cease till the revolution arrives, striking slavery into dust, elevating liberty to the throne. Whenever a people arise for its freedom, whenever that seed of liberty gets germinated in the blood of its fathers, whenever there remains at least one true son to avenge that blood of his fathers, there never can be an end to such a war as this.[21]

Savarkar reiterated many of these sentiments in the introduction to his book. Almost echoing Chattopadhyay, he wrote, 'The nation that has no consciousness of its past has no future. Equally true it is that a nation must develop its capacity not only of claiming a past but also of knowing how to use it for the furtherance of its future. The nation ought to be the master and not the slave of its own history.'[22] There are at least three interrelated points that need to be highlighted here. One was that the past that the British had appropriated needed to be rightfully reappropriated by Indians. Second, the past must be used as an inspiration to shape the future. Third, the past would be an inspiration only when it was interpreted in a particular way. Savarkar had no doubt in his mind about the trajectory of his interpretation: 'Out of the heap of ashes [in his mind] appeared forth sparks of a fiery inspiration.' The 'mutiny of 1857', as the British called it, had shining within it a 'War of Independence'.[23] The warriors in that war were all martyrs and among them was Lakshmibai.

Having elevated Lakshmibai to a martyr, Savarkar did not feel the need to absolve her of her involvement in the massacre at Jhansi in June 1857. He described the incident and added a footnote as well: 'There is an authoritative work on the life of the Queen of Jhansi by a well-known Marathi historian, and there the able author has established by an incontestable array of proofs that there was not the least incitement to this massacre from the young Queen. This work has had a wide circulation and is translated in other vernaculars in India, and so we think it unnecessary to repeat the argument once more.'[24] The 'authoritative work' by 'a well-known Marathi historian' is of course none other than the book published by Parasnis in 1894—a book to which Savarkar referred to a number of times. It is important to note that Parasnis's book did not contain 'an incontestable array of proofs' except the letter from Martin to Damodar Rao, which no other writer, scholar or historian ever saw. Parasnis's major argument was not based on Martin's letter but on the claim that there was no documentary evidence that Lakshmibai had been implicated in the massacre. But all this was not of any consequence to Savarkar, committed as he was to producing a eulogy for the martyr.

Savarkar described her career and her death in battle and then proceeded to apotheosize her:

On the pyre, if not on the throne! But Lakshmibai is still with her sweetheart Liberty! She has forced open the gates of death by falling in battle and has now entered the other world. Pursuit can no longer harm her . . . Thus fought Lakshmi. She had achieved her purpose, fulfilled her ambition, carried out her resolve! One such life vindicates the whole existence of a nation. She was the concentrated essence of all virtues. A mere woman, hardly twenty-three yet (sic), beautiful as rose, charming in her manners, pure of conduct, she had a power of organization of her subjects, exhibited by very few, even among men. The flame of patriotism was always burning in her heart. And she proud of her country's honour and pre-eminent in war! It is very rarely that a nation is so fortunate as to be able to claim such an angelic person, as a daughter and a queen.

So rare was Lakshmibai as an individual that such a person was not known in the history of England, and even in the 'Revolution of Italy', where 'high ideals and heroism of the very highest type are to be found', such an individual was unknown—'Italy could not give birth to Lakshmi.'[25]

The process of deification is indicated by the dropping of the suffix *bai* from Lakshmibai; as Lakshmi, she was the very embodiment of all virtues—beauty, charm, ability, patriotism and purity. She was the pride of India. But the exposition of these virtues became possible because of the 'glorious War of Independence'. Savarkar's rhetoric continued: 'The precious pearls in the ocean are not to be found on its surface. The Suryakanta jewel does not give out flames in the quiet of the night; nor does the flint give up its spark on soft cushions. They want resistance. Injustice makes the mind restless . . . every drop of blood must actually boil; intense national feeling is thus set aflame in such a furnace, the particles of virtue begin to flow . . . the concentrated essence of virtues begins to appear.' The battle thus continued even as heroic warriors fell: 'Everywhere battle and thunder-storms! A veritable volcanic conflagration this! And the pyre, flaming near the cottage of Gangadas Bawa, is the last and the most lustrous flame of this raging volcanic conflagration of the War of Independence of 1857.'[26]

The cremation place of Lakshmibai had thus become holy ground with a flame that could never be put out. In the powerful rhetoric of Savarkar, Lakshmibai, as Lakshmi, stepped out of history as an inspiring myth.

It was but a short step from myth to fiction. In 1946, the well-known novelist and political activist Vrindavanlal Varma wrote a novel called *Jhansi ki Rani* (The Queen of Jhansi).[27] It remains even today the most powerful fictional account of Lakshmibai's life and career. Varma was born in 1889 and had a very long and distinguished life; he died in 1969, having witnessed and participated in many important milestones of Indian history and politics. He was from Jhansi and his grandfather had been a rebel in 1857. In his early thirties, Varma became involved in politics and began writing. He joined the Liberal Party and was thus a constitutional moderate and a critic of Gandhian mass movements. He served on the Jhansi district local board from 1936 to 1952; from Jhansi he stood to be a member of India's first Lok Sabha in 1952 but lost the election. In spite of his multi-faceted career, Varma is remembered as a writer, especially of historical novels, among which *Jhansi ki Rani* has pride of place. One of the significant features of this novel was the fact that it was steeped in very deep historical research. Varma's narrative blurred the distinction between history and fiction, bestowing on his novel the simulacrum of authenticity. He depended heavily on Parasnis's book; he was convinced, however, that there were more elements to add to his story than the known facts. Like Savarkar, he was dismayed by the biases inherent in British accounts. Varma wrote that in Jhansi he had probed and pushed the memories of many old men to discover more about Lakshmibai and what had happened in Jhansi in 1857. He had the literary skill and the imagination to use the known historical facts and people's recollections of things past to construct a narrative that was not only convincing but a representation of reality. Such was its compelling power that historians have actually used it as an authentic source, overlooking the fact that it was actually a novel.[28]

Needless to say, the tone of Varma's novel was celebratory. Lakshmibai was a heroine: This was the raison d'être of Varma's novel. He narrated how, when the British were trapped in the Jhansi fort, on the second day they asked Lakshmibai to help them as they had completely run out of food. She had rotis prepared for them and asked two of her most trusted retainers to take them to the British through secret routes. One of the retainers asked Lakshmibai, 'My lady, would the British have helped us had we been in their place?' Lakshmibai replied: 'Why become like them?'[29] Varma thus placed Lakshmibai on a moral high ground compared to the British: The latter lacked humanity, but Lakshmibai was a humane queen. Lakshmibai, in Varma's rendering of her life story, was part of a wider conspiracy—an idea made popular by Savarkar—to fight the British. In the above incident, in her reply to the retainer's question, Varma has her say, 'Moreover, I don't want to spoil our future plans by starving them now.' In a similar vein, when Lakshmibai wrote to the British seeking permission to perform her son's *upanayana* or sacred thread ceremony, she was, according to Varma, sending out a covert message to the rebel leaders for a meeting.[30] A conspiracy provided the context for a dramatic interpretation of a simple letter of request to a higher authority, whose subsidiary Lakshmibai was. Under Lakshmibai's rule, Jhansi was a place where Hindus and Muslims lived together in peace, and members of both communities loved and respected her. Lakshmibai herself was the epitome of piety and respected all faiths.[31] To drive home this point, Varma has a Muslim soldier, at the end of the novel, protect the ground where Lakshmibai has been cremated. The soldier prevents the desecration of the spot by declaring it the site of a Muslim saint.[32] The cremation ground of an 'angelic' (Savarkar's evocative adjective) queen acquired thus a sacred aura. In Varma's eyes, 'The Rani fought for Swarajya, died for Swarajya and turned herself into a stone for the foundation of Swarajya.'[33] Thus was Lakshmibai consecrated.

If a Hindi writer could produce a powerful novel on Lakshmibai, could a Bengali author be far behind? In 1956, a year before the centenary, Maheaweta Bhattacharjee (she would later be better known as Mahasweta Devi) wrote a book that replicated in Bengali the title of Varma's novel.[34] In the preface, she thanked Varma for his help with research. She stated in the preface that her book was not history in the conventional sense but a humble attempt to draw the life and the character of the Rani of Jhansi. Perhaps what she meant to indicate was that her book was not a work of history in that it was not based on the kind of archival empirical evidence that historians rely on. She drew extensively on folk songs, folk memories and the lore about Lakshmibai that lived on in Jhansi even ninety-eight years after her death. That statement about her death, if one were to go by the stories and traditions that Bhattacharjee discovered, was problematic. Common people in Jhansi refused to accept that Lakshmibai was dead; she was still among them—she could still be seen on moonlit nights on the ramparts of the fort. '*Rani margay na howni, abhi to jinda howy*'—the common people repeatedly told the writer. Bhattacharjee wrote, 'So where is Rani Lakshmibai? To get her, you have to go to those places, to know those human beings who believe to this day from the depths of their hearts that their baisahib is not dead. She is hiding somewhere. Then from the beliefs of these uneducated, poor peasants will emerge a remarkable woman, an amazing woman/daughter of this India. If one could get out the inner truth of India and give it a form that would be Rani Lakshmibai.' To know this one would have to go to the Bundelkhand of the 1850s and one would have to know Jhansi. But Bhattacharjee reminded her readers that such a visit would have to be made with the mindset of a pilgrim. This is how the opening chapter of the book, 'Context', invoked Lakshmibai. But that invocation in the last paragraph of the chapter moved beyond the people of Jhansi—'The people of India have not recognized her death.' Lakshmibai was a living presence in Jhansi. She was immortal in India.

It would not be incorrect or unfair to say that the purpose of Bhattacharjee's book was to trace the path of Lakshmibai's journey to immortality. Bhattacharjee blends seamlessly the many stories about Lakshmibai with historical documentation. This makes her narrative layered, and it is often difficult to locate the points at which it moves from lore to documents. Not unexpectedly, she dismisses any possibility of Lakshmibai's involvement, or even complicity, in the massacre of the white people in Jhansi. On one very significant point she departs from Savarkar: She writes that Lakshmibai was not a part of any plot or conspiracy regarding the revolt.[35] If she was not a player in a grand plot, what were the elements, apart from the well-known fact that she embraced death in the manner of a true soldier, that contributed to her immortality? Here Bhattacharjee emphasizes the following aspects in Lakshmibai's story. As wife to a king, she was surrounded by Hindu servants, friends and relatives. She was quick to comprehend that in a crisis it would be impossible to work with such a small group. In difficult times, many people were needed: those who would defend Jhansi with their lives. Such commitment could only come from the people of Bundelkhand. So she called upon them. From Bundela *thakurs* to *kachhi*, *kori*, *teli*, people from all castes and communities joined her army. She simultaneously appealed to and brought in Afghans, Pathans and other Muslims. Her trust in all these people inspired them and earned her their loyalty. Cutting across religion and caste, she formed an army of women who were taught to shoot, use the sword and ride horses. They were trained to help men in the firing of cannons. Lakshmibai and her army of women had joined the battle against the foreign enemy. This is proof, Bhattacharjee writes, of Lakshmibai's consciousness to fight and resist. 'Our country has many instances of brave heroines, but the rani's role was more complete and meaningful than the others.'

Hindus and Muslims rallied under the flag of Lakshmibai: 'Every heart was touched by enthusiasm and inspiration. Every home produced soldiers. This is why the rani is truly a great leader. A successful leader does not just elevate herself, with her she lifts thousands of other lives, builds thousands of warriors. The rani passed this test and that is why her leadership was the most successful.' Dressed in a Pathan costume she rode around the city, working with the people and giving them instructions. Everyone could see that their rani was toiling with them. Her interactions with the soldiers were captured in a folk song, which Bhattacharjee said was still sung by old peasants: 'The rani fed the sipahis *malai* (cream), but she herself ate *gur* (molasses) and *khoi* (dried rice).'[36]

Bhattacharjee did not evade the issue of Lakshmibai's letters to Erskine. She wrote that these letters had been interpreted by Maharashtrian biographers (Bhattacharjee did not name any) to show that she had initially been loyal to the British, and only when her loyalty was questioned did she decide to fight them. Bhattacharjee offered a different reading. She argued that in the early stages, the rebellion had been confined to north India. Jhansi was in central India where there was no scent of rebellion. All around were thakurs who were against Jhansi. The neighbouring Maratha principalities like Indore and Gwalior were allies of the British. The Begum of Bhopal was well known for her loyalty to the British. At that stage, it was not clear that opposition to foreign rule would acquire the scale of a massive resistance. Under these circumstances, Lakshmibai realized that if she declared war against the British, the responsibility for defeating them would fall to her and the condition of Jhansi would worsen. These considerations made her approach Erskine to inform him of what was going on in. Perhaps she thought that when these disparate acts of rebellion came to an end, the British would understand her role and recognize her son's claims to be the ruler of Jhansi. After Erskine asked Lakshmibai to rule Jhansi, he found out that Canning believed Lakshmibai to be guilty of the massacre. Erskine then began to play a double role. He incited the Rani of Orcha to attack Jhansi. But Lakshmibai was quick to discern this game. She abandoned diplomacy and chose the battlefield. She unfurled her own flag in Jhansi.

About the flag Bhattacharjee had this to say:

Once the flag of the Maratha empire had been of saffron colour. Saffron is the colour of forgiveness and sacrifice. But this colour had failed to cast any influence on the mind of the rani. She had by then wagered her 22-year-old life to fight the foreign power. She had decided that there, only one language would be used to talk to them—the language of the flashing sword and the roar of the cannon. The only ground on which they would stand would be the battlefield and they would treat each other as an enemy treats an enemy . . . if in these critical times the rani's mind bore no signs of forgiveness and sacrifice, can she be blamed for that? So she unfurled the red flag on the southern battlement of the fort. The sky of 1857 was then red. The whole of Central India was in the grip of protest . . . That red flag flew proudly on the fort of Jhansi as the symbol of the resistance of lakhs of Indian people. That flag flew till Hugh Rose's troops tore it down.[37]

Bhattacharjee did not spell out the implications of the red flag (if it was at all unfurled on top of the Jhansi fort) and why she gave to it so much importance. It is worth mentioning that Bhattacharjee in 1956 was close to the undivided Communist Party of India and that her then husband Bijon Bhattacharjee— to whom she dedicated her book—was an outstanding actor, theatre director and one of the leading personalities in the Indian People's Theatre Association. Was Bhattacharjee, by invoking the red flag, implicitly trying to pull Lakshmibai away from Maratha nationalism and appropriating her to a different kind of ideology? If indeed that was her purpose, then it sits very uneasily with the way she ended the book. She wrote, 'Her memory is immortal. Memory is in the minds of human beings. *Puja* (worship) is in the hearts of people. So one's head bows in *bhakti* (devotion) when her life is recalled.'[38]

Bhattacharjee had invited her readers at the beginning of the book to visit Jhansi as a pilgrim. She saw Lakshmibai as someone worthy of puja and bhakti. She was more than a human being. She had been transformed in the prose of powerful writers into an icon. Icons never die.

An icon needs an anthem.[39] For Lakshmibai it came from the poet Subhadra Kumari Chauhan. An ardent nationalist who participated in Gandhian mass movements, she wrote a ballad on Lakshmibai that is one of the most famous poems in Hindi literature in its particular genre. Its mood and its language are stirring. Its aim is to inspire. Through her verses and the ways in which they are recited in high school elocution contests and on other occasions, the name, the courage and the achievements of Lakshmibai have become enshrined in public memory. There was one salient feature in the way Subhadra Kumari Chauhan memorialized Lakshmibai. She drew on folk traditions about her. As already noted, the oft-quoted refrain of her poem *Khoob lari mardani, woh to Jhansi wali Rani thi* echoed a popular folk song.[40] Another refrain, occurring at the end of every verse, like the line just quoted above, stressed on folk memory: '*Bundele harbolon ke munh hamne suni kahani thi'* ('From the mouths of Bundela Harbolas we heard the tale').'[41] Drawing on folklore, the poet assumed the divine status of Lakshmibai as a given: '*Lakshmi thi ya Durga thi swyam veerta ki avatar'* (No one could guess whether she was Lakshmi or Durga, she was the incarnation of bravery'). Subhadra Kumari's paean to Lakshmibai's divinity reaches a crescendo in the penultimate verse:

> *Rani gayee sidhaar chita ab uski divya sawaari thi,*
> *mila tej se tej, tej ki woh sachchi adhikaari thi,*
> *abhi umr kul teis ki thi, manuj nahin avtaari thi . . .*

(Her departed soul was then riding a divine vehicle moving towards the heavens/ The light of her divine soul met with the divine light in the heavens, she was the real heir of divinity.') The people of India, the poet said, will remember this debt of yours.

Mahasweta Bhattacharjee, who wrote many years after Subhadra Kumari had composed her hymn to Lakshmibai, was only echoing the poet when she depicted Lakshmibai as someone who deserved worship and devotion. From anecdote to anthem and to more prosaic forms of expression, Lakshmibai had traversed a path where she was an able queen, a brave warrior and a martyr. That journey's end was the recognition of her as an incarnation of divinity—to be remembered with puja and bhakti. She had thus entered the Indian pantheon of icons and mythical figures.

The way Lakshmibai is revered and remembered is in sharp contrast to the remembrance of Hazrat Mahal. It is not that the latter is effaced from history. Rather, she is not given the kind of attention and importance that was and is still accorded to Lakshmibai. To an extent this neglect is derived from the nineteenth-century British historians who described Lakshmibai as a heroic adversary but did not use such accolades for Hazrat Mahal. Indian academic historians in the centenary year followed this trend. R.C. Majumdar in his book has a section called 'Heroes'. Hazrat Mahal does not feature there; Lakshmibai, of course, does, as does Maulavi Ahmadullah Shah. Unwittingly or otherwise, writers on 1857 seem to have set up a hierarchy of heroes in which Hazrat Mahal was many rungs lower than Lakshmibai.

A hierarchy of heroes is suggested by Savarkar, who in his influential book devoted one chapter to 'Oudh' and another to 'Lucknow'. In the latter he wrote, 'This Begum of Oudh [Hazrat Mahal], *though not quite another Lakshmi Bai*, was undoubtedly a great organizer, full of love of liberty and the spirit of daring [italics mine].'[42] This statement is appreciative of Hazrat Mahal's courage, her qualities as an organizer and as an upholder of freedom (Savarkar, as we shall see in the next paragraph, detailed her organizational and administrative skills) but is unwilling to place her at the same level as Lakshmibai. Savarkar did not say where Hazrat Mahal—who was also brave, a fighter for liberty and an able administrator—fell short in comparison to Lakshmibai. The italicized phrase in the above quotation thus hangs as an enigma. It would be utterly erroneous to say that Savarkar was making this comparative statement on the basis of his religious predilections. In 1909, when the book was published, Savarkar had not yet emerged as the principal ideologue of Hindutva that he was later to become. His book on 1857 argued that Hindus and Muslims had fought together in the war of independence. In fact, in his introduction to the book, Savarkar noted very pointedly, 'The feeling of hatred against the Mahomedans was just and necessary in the times of Shivaji—but such a feeling would be unjust and foolish if nursed now, simply because it was the dominant feeling of the Hindus then.' According to Savarkar, hatred of the Muslims was an emotion arising out of a particular historical conjuncture. In the early twentieth century, as in 1857, such sectarian emotions were unfair and irrelevant. Savarkar thus had no hesitation in devoting a full chapter to Maulavi Ahmadullah Shah (he called him 'Moulvie Ahmad Shah'). This only makes his non-inclusion of Hazrat Mahal in his gallery of heroes more complex, if not incomprehensible. This almost complete erasure of Hazrat Mahal is particularly bewildering given the fact that she became a rebel long before Lakshmibai and remained one even after Lakshmibai had met her death on the battlefield.

Describing the actions of Hazrat Mahal, Savarkar wrote how she went about appointing various officers to the judicial, revenue, police and military departments. He added, 'These officers selected were such as were loved and honoured by the representatives of the Sepoys, by Mahbub Khan [Savarkar noted that Hazrat Mahal had 'perfect confidence' in him] and other leading Sirdars, and also by the large numbers of the people who hurried from all parts of Oudh to Lucknow to join the great War of Independence.' Savarkar went on to say that every day Hazrat Mahal held a durbar to discuss political affairs and 'there the Begum Sahiba exercised authority in the name of the Nabob. The news that Oudh was free and that not a trace of English rule remained there was sent to the Emperor of Delhi, under the Begum's seal, along with valuable presents.'[43] Hazrat

Mahal, Savarkar wrote, sent letters to all the neighbouring zamindars and vassal rajas to come to Lucknow with armed followers. According to Savarkar, 'From the appointment of the various civil officers, from the good order in all the departments of Government, from the daily Durbars, and other signs, it was apparent that the revolt had ended and constructive government had begun.'[44] In his appreciation of the role of Hazrat Mahal, Savarkar did not include the fact that she had actually drawn up battle plans and deployment of troops. Hazrat Mahal was a military leader, not just an administrator. What no book or document mentioned is whether she was physically present on the battlefield and joined the military action. This is an unknown, whereas for Lakshmibai there is clear and abundant evidence that she not only planned but actually fought. It is entirely possible that military valour as displayed on the field of battle made Savarkar and other writers place Lakshmibai above Hazrat Mahal in the hierarchy of heroes.

As suggested earlier on in this chapter, this calibration of heroes was possibly derived from the way common people remembered Lakshmibai and Hazrat Mahal. The former was celebrated and revered in songs remembered by common peasants in Jhansi one hundred years after her death. But Hazrat Mahal was remembered only in one verse of a song; and that verse too was somewhat ambivalent. One part of the verse eulogized her:

What kind of bravery did Birjis Qadr, the Queen show
Her name has remained in the world
Who will ever show such courage?

But the last line tempered the praise: 'When the Queen had fled what fight was possible?'[45] The verse captured the moods of celebration and lament together. These folk recollections, along with the writings of British generals and British historians, left their imprint on the way Indian historians viewed and evaluated Lakshmibai and Hazrat Mahal. S.N. Sen's history of the revolt, written in the centenary year, is a narrative that does not seek out heroes. But he devotes substantially more space to Lakshmibai than he does to Hazrat Mahal. For the latter, he does not provide the overall summing up and evaluation that he does for the former. Sen's history bears out the point I am trying to make here about folk recollections and the remembrance of British officers. Sen wrote: '. . . the Rani died in the battlefield a soldier's death. Next to Nana, she was probably the person most hated by her enemies . . . If the reverence of her own people is any compensation for vilification by her enemies the Rani of Jhansi stands more than vindicated. Thousands of unsophisticated villagers still sing of the valour and virtues of the woman who held her own against the Bundela enemies to fall under a British bullet.'[46] How common people remember and do not remember became the basis of the evaluation of educated nationalist leaders and historians.[47]

Were there any other factors than military valour that influenced how Lakshmibai and Hazrat Mahal were remembered, evaluated and written about? Answers to this question will be by necessity somewhat speculative, but the issues need to be addressed. Lakshmibai's extraordinary courage is well documented and noted, as are her initial reluctance to join the rebellion and her efforts to reach out to the British authorities for assistance. Hazrat Mahal, on the other hand, embraced the rebellion immediately after the victory at Chinhat and remained the principal leader and planner of the rebellion in Awadh. Over and above this, the ishtahars issued in her or her son's name or under their respective seals contained some of the most potent critiques of British rule and the most powerful rejection of the Queen's Proclamation. Is it possible that the remembrance and the evaluation of the two are linked to their respective backgrounds and origins?

Lakshmibai was a Brahmin; her father was in the service of the Peshwa. She was not born into wealth, but her father had the resources to educate her and to train her in horse riding and the use of arms. She was married into minor royalty, and following the death of her husband, she was forced to take over the administration of Jhansi. By all accounts, she was an able and a generous ruler. But it is significant that when Hugh Rose praised her and spoke of the loyalty she commanded, he emphasized her 'high descent'. Lakshmibai's lineage, both in terms of caste and royalty, was important. Hazrat Mahal's origins were altogether different. Her beginnings were humble and somewhat unclear. She was, as noted in Chapter 1, the daughter of an African slave; her good looks and talents as a dancer caught the eyes of Wajid Ali Shah, who made her into a muta wife. When she gave birth to a son, she was elevated to the position of begum and then divorced. Out of her own choice or because of Wajid Ali Shah's decision, she remained in Lucknow and did not accompany the king to Calcutta. She was a slave's daughter who, by a stroke of fortune, became a begum, only to lose that status through a divorce and again to regain it through a rebellion against the British. The sharp contrast between her position and that of Lakshmibai can be put across through a counter fact. If the rebellion of 1857 had not happened, Hazrat Mahal would have been a nobody. The revolt gave her a place in history: it enabled her to emerge as a leader who fought the British through arms and words but eventually had to flee and embrace an anonymity similar to that of her origins. The revolt of 1857 made her. But in the case of Lakshmibai, even if the rebellion had not erupted, she would have been queen of Jhansi. The rebellion made her visible as a soldier and military leader and eventually as a martyr. When, in the course of the rising tide of nationalism, there was a search for a nationalist icon and the nationalists harked back to 1857, Hazrat Mahal was not even a candidate. Lakshmibai was the obvious choice.

The word 'obvious' at the end of the last paragraph is deliberately used: obvious in the sense of 'natural', a choice dictated by common sense. But the choice was not unproblematic. Who were the people that nominated Lakshmibai to her unique place in the pantheon of Indian nationalism? The nominators were a varied group—from Savarkar to Subhas Bose to Jawaharlal Nehru to novelists and poets and historians. There must have been some discrimination at work here—some unstated values—that made her rise above other claimants. It could not have been just her gender, since Hazrat Mahal was also a woman. Was it because these nominators did not know about Hazrat Mahal? Not really. Savarkar wrote about her in appreciative terms but placed her below Lakshmibai. What influenced the choice was the ideology of nationalism that privileged the explicit and outward show of valour—a nationalism that was also looking for inspirational exemplars. Indian nationalism was also seeking to project a new construct of woman—one who stood as a sign for 'nation' and embodied the 'spiritual qualities of self-sacrifice, benevolence, devotion, religiosity and so on.'[48] Lakshmibai easily fitted the bill of virtues; valour was an additional quality. The fact that Lakshmibai was a Brahmin and a benevolent queen cannot be eliminated as factors that influenced the choice. An upper caste queen was preferable to a Muslim dancing girl who was the daughter of an African slave. This is not to suggest that the choice was pre-meditated and deliberately prejudiced. 'Prejudice', as Gyanendra Pandey has noted, 'is not proclaimed from the rooftops . . . It is hardly self-conscious. It appears instead as common sense, as the natural order of things: what is, is— and, if all were properly ordered, must be.'[49] In a national movement that was largely male- and upper caste-dominated, it was 'the natural order of things' to iconize Lakshmibai and not efface Hazrat Mahal but relegate her. The quest for heroes in history creates its own problems of choice and discrimination.

*

In spite of the many contrasts that I have drawn out, there were some similarities in the experiences of Hazrat Mahal and Lakshmibai, since both grew up in the male-dominated world of the early nineteenth century. For both, the journey of becoming a woman was unusual for the time. For one thing, neither of them was a child bride, as would have been customary at the time among Hindus and Muslims. Lakshmibai—given that she was probably born, as suggested in Chapter 1, in 1829 or 1830—was in her early teens when she was married to Gangadhar Rao in the early 1840s. Hazrat Mahal, too, was most likely a teenager when she became the muta wife of Wajid Ali Shah and entered his harem in 1845. By this time, she was already at the music school known (Pari Khana) where she came to be called Mahak Pari. Admittedly, the dates given are a trifle speculative, but the speculation is not entirely baseless. Some other unusual aspects of their coming to being as women need to be highlighted. Lakshmibai became skilled in the use of arms and was a capable equestrian. Most women in the early nineteenth century, especially those who came from backgrounds similar to Lakshmibai's, were not trained in these skills. Even though Hazrat Mahal was an African slave's daughter, she was sent to a music school— the most famous one in Lucknow, no less. This too was remarkable given her background. She must have displayed in the Pari Khana some exceptional artistic talent to have been noticed by the king.

It might be appropriate to introduce here the notion of playfulness, which was elucidated by Ruby Lal in the most original and suggestive way in her book on how women came of age in the nineteenth century in north India.[50] Lal suggested that girls transitioning to womanhood were inclined to gravitate towards spheres marked by 'creativity, almost an art of taking initiative within restrictive circumstances and domain'.[51] It was through the art of playfulness carried out in a range of actual physical spaces—ranging from the forest to the rooftop—that women in the nineteenth century began the process of demarcating and exercising their autonomy, albeit under severely restrictive and orthodox circumstances. For Lakshmibai, the horse-riding training ground and the arena where she was taught swordsmanship can easily be pinned down as spaces where she learnt to become a woman. Playfulness was even more integral to Hazrat Mahal's coming into her own. She joined an academy for music in Lucknow, where under Wajid Ali Shah's patronage, dancing, music, performance and other forms of entertainment and arts of pleasure were acquiring an unprecedented prominence. She became a courtesan—a profession where erotic pleasure was also a form of play. In Lucknow, courtesans blurred the distinction between respectability and prostitution: an aristocratic gentleman enhanced his respectability by enjoying the company of courtesans or even by keeping one special courtesan for his own pleasure.[52]

When circumstances bestowed on Lakshmibai and Hazrat Mahal responsibilities and activities that were traditionally seen as being 'male' preserves, they were not entirely unprepared. Their training had made them acquire very distinct qualities and identities. The world in which they had been born had not fully opened up to the possibilities—though through playfulness they had had a glimpse of them—of 'whut a woman oughta be and to do'.[53] But the embrace of a popular uprising that thrust upon them leadership roles made them fulfil the dream—and dare one add for women of the future too—of what a woman ought to be and ought to do.

Lakshmibai and Hazrat Mahal had minor sons who accompanied their mothers as they led the revolt against the British. Damodar Rao was about ten years old when his mother died. Birjis Qadr was around twelve when his mother took him to Nepal as a fugitive. It occurred to neither woman to abandon her son. While in Nepal, Hazrat Mahal was offered a pension that would be independent of what was being paid to her former husband Wajid Ali Shah; she was also assured of honours that suited her rank. She spurned the offers and stayed on and died in Nepal.[54] After her death, on the occasion of the golden jubilee of Queen Victoria ascending the throne, Birjis Qadr was pardoned; he returned to India and went to Calcutta, where he died of food poisoning.[55] There are no reasons to assume that his life in Nepal was in any way comfortable. After the revolt had been suppressed in Bundelkhand, Rao roamed around the neighbourhood of Jhansi appealing to the government to be pardoned and be paid a pension. In 1860, his appeals bore fruit. The British government decided to grant him a pension of Rs 150 per month.[56] There was something apposite here, that Lakshmibai, before she turned a rebel, had been a pensioner of the British government and her son too became a pensioner of the Raj. Hazrat Mahal received no favours from the British: She had spurned a pension and honours. Her son too died without British patronage.

*

History, to invoke a line from one of Shakespeare's sonnets, is a remembrance of things past. But the past is never remembered, and cannot be, in its entirety. History is stalked by incompleteness—what is chosen to be remembered, and what does not earn a niche in collective memory. Forgetting is as much a part of the muse of Clio as remembering. Lakshmibai is not only remembered, but also commemorated and celebrated. Hazrat Mahal hovers on the margins of remembrance.

APPENDIX TO CHAPTER 2

A NOTE ON VISHNU BHATT GODSE'S
MAJHA PRAVAS

One of the problems that historians face when studying the revolt of 1857 is the paucity of accounts emanating from the Indian side. This issue has been discussed in the Introduction. In this context, readers familiar with the literature on 1857, especially the part that pertains to Jhansi, may have noticed that I do not use a particular Marathi text that claims to be a first-hand account of the revolt in Jhansi. This is *Majha Pravas: Athrashesattavan chya Bandachi Hakikat* (My Travels: A History of the 1857 Revolt) by Vishnu Bhatt Godse, which was published in 1907. It was translated into Hindi in 1948 by Amritlal Nagar as *Ankhon Dekha Gadar: Vishnu Bhatt krit Maza Pravas ka Hindi Anuvaad* (An Eyewitness to the Revolt: a Hindi Translation of Vishnubhat Godse's *Maza Pravaas*). An English translation of this work was made by Mrinal Pande and entitled *1857: The Real Story of the Uprising* (Delhi: Harper, Perennial: 2011). I follow here Pande's translation. The value and importance of *Maza Pravas* are enhanced by the claim that it is an eyewitness account. This note will try and assess that claim and justify why it has not been used as documentary evidence in my reconstruction of the events in Jhansi.

A few words are first in order about the provenance of the text. The author was a Chitpavan Brahmin from Alibagh in the Kolaba district near what is now Mumbai. Vishnu Bhatt used to wax eloquent about his experiences in north India during the uprising. A client of his asked him to write down his experiences. So twenty-four years after the experiences had actually taken place, Bhatt wrote them down. He did not want his account published till after his death. Thus it was not published till 1907. The printed version did not escape editorial emendations. The friend who had asked Bhatt to write and to whom Bhatt had given the manuscript for safekeeping—a man called Chintamani Vinayak Vaidya, a practitioner of traditional medicine—decided to omit certain sections that he considered unnecessary. According to Mrinal Pande: 'He felt that he should reshape the book to make it seem like a work of fiction'. We don't know if Bhatt would have approved of such changes since he died in 1903. The original manuscript had no chapter divisions. However, the author signed off wherever a particular series of events ended.

This short introduction makes one thing obvious. Even if the book was an eyewitness account, it lacked the quality of immediacy since it was written many years after the events it recounted. Indeed, Bhatt's book was a feat of memory. It would be interesting to locate where memory had served to filter or even distort history.

One problem with Bhatt's narrative is dates. The first chapter, which recalls his early life and his journey to north India, has very precise dates, all given in the Saka era. Thus he says he began his journey on Tuesday, *panchami*, the fifth day of the bright lunar fortnight in the month of Phalguna. The year was Saka 1778. This would mean sometime in February–March 1856. Another precise date is in the section on Jhansi, where Bhatt writes, 'On 9 June 1857, a day before the mutiny began . . .' Did Bhatt actually mention the date following the western calendar? Could an orthodox Brahmin in the middle of the nineteenth century have been familiar with dates in the western calendar? Or is this the translator's addition? If yes, what was the actual date mentioned by Bhatt? According to all available documentation, the sepoys mutinied in Jhansi on 5–6 June 1857. How did Bhatt arrive at the date of June 10 as the onset of the mutiny in Jhansi?

The section on Jhansi and Bundelkhand is preceded by one on Gwalior, Kanpur and Lucknow. The uprising began in Lucknow on 31 May and in Kanpur on 4 June. If we are to accept that Bhatt was an eyewitness to the events in Lucknow and Kanpur, then he could not have been present in Jhansi when the mutiny began there on 5–6 June. One of the two sections is based on hearsay. In fact, a reading of the section on Lucknow and Kanpur reveals that Bhatt was not an eyewitness to the events. As someone who has done some research on the revolt of 1857 in Lucknow and Kanpur, I can say that Bhatt's account bristles with too many inconsistencies to have the ring of authenticity.

On Jhansi, the reader is on somewhat firmer ground. But here too, one should be careful to distinguish between what Bhatt saw and what Bhatt heard. For example, Bhatt's retelling of the Rani of Jhansi's early life and the history of pre-annexation Jhansi could not have been based on first-hand knowledge. He must have heard it from someone, maybe from more than one person. Is the account then authentic?

In his recounting of the uprising in Jhansi, Bhatt writes, 'On 9 June 1857, a day before the mutiny began, Gordon Sahib sent a message to the Rani that she should assume charge of Jhansi city.' And he goes on to add that later that evening Gordon—who Bhatt mistakenly calls the Resident; he was the deputy superintendent of Jhansi—came to see Lakshmibai to tell her that his wife was seven months pregnant and appealed to her to save his wife and unborn child. Bhatt writes, 'The rani heard him out and, being a noble soul, finally promised to protect the women and children of the British. Gordon Sahib went back and, at seven the next morning, the women and children from the British families came and took shelter under the rani's roof.' There are a number of problems with this account. First, all documentary evidence says that Gordon was shot through the head on 8 June. Second, if Lakshmibai gave shelter to the British women and children, how did they come to be massacred? Did she hand them over to the rebels? There is no evidence that she did either. Bhatt's memory was obviously deceiving him when he sat down to recollect and write down what had happened in Jhansi. Equally surprising is that he does not mention anywhere that after having fought and killed the Britons, the sepoys sped off towards Delhi.

Bhatt claims to have been in Jhansi between the middle of June 1857 till Hugh Rose's attack on Jhansi in late March 1858 and the fall of Jhansi in April. His account of this period is first-hand but is mostly about Lakshmibai's daily life, her piousness and general tittle-tattle about Jhansi. He claims repeatedly that he met Lakshmibai on several occasions, but he never once describes what she looked like. This is a strange omission and enough to raise an eyebrow about the account's authenticity.

The inconsistencies in Bhatt's narrative have made historians of 1857 sceptical about its value. S.N. Sen, the author of *1857*, who knew Marathi, listed the book in his bibliography but did not use it extensively. This was because much of what Bhatt wrote, even about Jhansi, cannot be corroborated against other sources. It is standard practice among historians to cross-check sources. Bhatt's text does not quite pass scrutiny. The text also bears too many signs of dependence on memory and hearsay to be given the status of an eyewitness account.

Bhatt was obviously a raconteur who charmed his friends and audiences when he narrated his experiences in north India in 1856–57. What he said was partly what he had himself seen and partly what he had heard as he moved across a vast terrain. Added to these was the act of recollection and all the tricks that human memory is prey to. Does all this make for a 'factual account' as Bhatt claimed? Historians will continue to be sceptical.

APPENDIX A TO CHAPTER 3

PROCLAMATION BY THE BEGUM OF OUDH

At this time certain weak-minded, foolish people have spread a report that the English have forgiven the faults and crimes of the people of Hindoostan. This appears very astonishing, for it is the unvarying custom of the English never to forgive a fault, be it great or small, so much so that if a small offence be committed through ignorance or negligence, they never forgive it. The proclamation of the 1st November, 1858, which has come before us, is perfectly clear; and as some foolish people, not understanding the real object of the proclamation, have been carried away, there we, the ever-abiding government, *parents of the people of Oude,* with great consideration, put forth the present proclamation, in order that the real object of the chief points may be exposed, and our subjects placed on their guard.

1. It is written in the proclamation that the country of Hindoostan, which was held in trust by the Company,

has been resumed by the Queen, and that for the future the Queen's laws shall be obeyed. This is not to be trusted by our religious subjects; for the laws of the Company, the settlement of the Company, the English servants of the Company, are all unchanged. What, then, is there now which can benefit the people, or on which [they] can rely?

2. In the proclamation it is written that all contracts and agreements entered into by the Company will be accepted by the Queen. *Let the people carefully observe this artifice.* The Company has seized on the whole of Hindoostan, and, if this arrangement be accepted, what is there new in it? *The Company professed to treat the Chief of Bhurtpore as a son, and then took his territory; the Chief of Lahore was carried off to London,* and it has not fallen to his lot to return; the Nawab Shumshoodeen Khan, on one side, they hanged, and on the other side, they salaamed to him; the Peishwa they expelled from Poona Sitara, and imprisoned for life in Bithoor; their breach of faith with Sultan Tippoo is well known; the Rajah of Benares they imprisoned in Agra. Under pretence of administering the country of the Chief of Gwalior, they introduced English customs; they have left no names or traces of the Chiefs of Behar, Orissa and Bengal; they gave the Rao of Furruckabad a small monthly allowance and took his territory. Shahjehanpore, Bareilly, Azimgurh, Jounpore, Goruckpore, Etawah, Allahabad, Futtehpore, &c. *Our ancient possessions they took from us on pretence of distributing pay; and in the 7th article of the treaty, they*

148

wrote, on oath, that they would take no more from us. If, then, the arrangements made by the Company are to be accepted, *what is the difference between the former and the present state of things?* These are old affairs, but recently, in defiance of treaties and oaths, and notwithstanding that they owed us millions of rupees without reason, and on pretence of this misconduct and discontent of our people, they took our country and property, worth millions of rupees. If our people were discontented with our royal predecessor, Wajid Ali Shah, how comes it they are content with us? And no ruler ever experienced such loyalty and devotion of life and goods as we have done. What, then, is wanting that they do not restore our country? Further, it is written in the proclamation that they want no increase of territory, but yet they cannot refrain from annexation. If the Queen has assumed the government, why does Her Majesty not restore our country to us when *our people wish it?* It is well-known that no king or queen ever punished a whole army and people for rebellion; all were forgiven; and the wise cannot approve of punishing the whole army and people of Hindoostan; for so long as the world punishment remains the disturbance will not be suppressed. There is a well-known proverb—'A dying man is desperate' (*Murta kya na kurta*). It is *impossible that a thousand should attach a million, and the thousand escape.*

3. In the proclamation it is written that the Christian religion is true, but that no other creed will suffer oppression, and that the laws will be observed towards all. *What has the administration of justice to do with the truth or falsehood of religion?* That religion is true which

acknowledges one God, and knows no other. Where there are three Gods in a religion, neither Mussulman nor Hindoos—nay, not even Jews, Sun-worshippers, or Fire-worshippers can believe it true. To eat pigs and drink wine—to bite greased cartridges, and to mix pig's fat with flour and sweetmeats—to destroy Hindoos and Mussalman temples on pretence of making roads to build churches—to send clergymen into the streets and alleys to preach the Christian religion—to institute English schools, and to pay a monthly stipend for learning the English sciences, while the places of worship of Hindoos and Mussalmans are to this day entirely neglected; with all this, how can the people believe that religion will not be interfered with? The rebellion began with religion, and, for it, millions of men have been killed. Let not our subjects be deceived; thousands were deprived of their religion in the North-West, and thousands were hanged rather than abandon their religion.

4. It is written in the proclamation that they who harboured rebels, or who were leaders of rebels, or who caused men to rebel, shall have their lives, but that punishment shall be awarded after deliberation, and that murderers and abettors of murderers shall have no mercy shown them, while all others shall be forgiven. *Any foolish person can see that under this proclamation, no one, be he guilty or innocent, can escape.* Everything is written, and yet nothing is written; but they have clearly written that they will not let off any one implicated; and in whatever village or estate the army may have halted, the inhabitants of that place cannot escape. We are deeply concerned for the condition of our people on reading this proclamation,

which palpably teems with enmity. We now issue a distinct order, and one that may be trusted that all subjects who may have foolishly presented themselves as heads of villages to the English, shall, before the 1st of January next, present themselves, in our camp. Without doubt their faults shall be forgiven them, and they shall be treated according to their merits. To believe in this proclamation *it is only necessary to remember that Hindoostanee rulers are altogether kind and merciful. Thousands have seen this, millions have heard it. No one has ever seen in a dream that the English forgave an offence.*

5. In this proclamation it is written that when peace is restored, public works, such as roads and canals, will be made in order to improve the condition of the people. It is worthy of a little reflection, that they have promised no better employment for Hindoostanees than making roads and digging canals. If people cannot see clearly what this means, there is no help for them. Let no subject be deceived by the proclamation.

APPENDIX B TO CHAPTER 3

Abstract Translation of an Urzee (Arzi) from the Rebel Camp on the part of all the rebel officers, sepoys &c. to Maharaja Jang Bahadur, bearing the Seals of (1st) Ram Bakhsh, General of First Division, (2nd) of Mansa Ram, Brigade Major, First Division, (3rd) of Ganga Singh, Lord, Nasirabad Division; no date.

We the *Nizamatee* and military, foot, cavalry, and artillery men, have all mutinied against the British, the reasons for which are as follows: A century ago the British arrived in Hindoostan and gradually entertained troops in their service, and became masters of every state. Our forefathers have always served them, and we also entered their service and we, as well as our children, have received every kind of support from the government of the Company and we also were ready to serve them and wish them well. By the mercy of God, and with our assistance the British also conquered every place they liked, in which thousands of us Hindoostani men were sacrificed, but we never made any excuses or pretences, nor revolted. Besides, our good acts towards the British are well known in every country. But in the year 1857 the British came out with an order that new cartridges and muskets which had arrived from England were to be issued—in the former, cow and pigfat was mixed; that attah of wheat mixed with powdered human bones was to be eaten and distributed in every Regiment of infantry, cavalry and artillery. In Meerut there were the 11th Regiment N.I., the 20th Regiment N.I., 3rd Light Cavalry. They gave these new cartridges to the sowars of the 3rd Light Cavalry, and ordered them to bite them; the troopers objected to it, and said that if they did, their religion and faith would be destroyed. There have been many kings in Hindoostan but none has taken our religion and faith. The British also have been in India about a century, but they have never befored acted in this manner. Upon this the British Officers paraded the men of the 3 Regiments and having prepared 1400 English soldiers, and other Battalions of European troops and Horse Artillery, surrounded them and placing 6 guns before each of the infantry regiments, loaded the guns with grape and made 84 new troopers prisoners, and put them placing 6 guns before each of the infantry regiments, loaded the guns with grape and made 84 new troopers prisoners, and put them in jail with irons on them. On this, we thought that if we also objected, our lives and faith would be destroyed for nothing—for which reason we fought with the British and went to Delhie. Prior to this, when the British had told Babu Koonwar Sing of Bhojepore to eat the wheat flour prepared by the government he had replied that he was a simple subject, but that when the men of the army, who were his brethren, had partaken of it, he would have no objection. The reason that the sowars of said cantonment were put into jail was that we should be frightened into biting the new cartridges; on this account we and all our countrymen having

united together, fought here and there with the British for
the preservation of our faith and not for the sake of treasure,
country, &c. The British say that we have only revolted for
treasure and country, and by such deceptions have prevailed
on those rajahs and chiefs to give them aid who do not pay a
single thought to faith or religion. The 7 *akleem*s (countries)
having risen on the misrepresentation of those against us,
we have been compelled to make war for two years and the
rajahs and chiefs who are with us in faith and religion are
still so, and have undergone all sorts of trouble; we have
fought for two years in order that our faith and religion not
be polluted. If the religion of a Hindoo or Mussalman is lost,
what remains in the world? We could not get any relief, for
the British received aid from all the rajahs and sirdars, because
of which no good resulted. To preserve our religion and faith
we have fought everywhere and undergone great troubles and
starvation (it is a long story) but no profit came through; now
we know that there is no one to preserve our faith, and the
British have with magic contrived to get everyone on their
side, and by giving large sums of money are endeavouring
to get us apprehended. We have now come to the conviction
that there is but one country of the Brahmanical thread left,
the remain (sic) of which is known throughout the country,
and we have heard from our forefathers, that whoever might
achieve a victory would be from the Northward. For this
reason we have, Hindoos and Mohamedans, come into your
territories that at all events some arrangements may be made
for us. In this hope, all the troops, rajahs and ilakadars, with
Her Gracious Majesty the begum, have come up to this place,
after undergoing starvation, and stumbling over the hills, in
the hope that should you protect our Brahmanical thread it

will be no wonder. God has made you master of a country at this time, and this increased our hopes in approaching your threshold. If the Rajah Sahib, taking our poor state into consideration, should preserve our faith and religion, God, who is glorious, will exalt his position; with this hope we have signed this *urzee* and sent it to you. May the sun of prosperity and wealth ever shine upon you. We hope for reply.

APPENDIX C TO CHAPTER 3

FATEH-I ISLAM AND A
PROCLAMATION INVOCATION

Praise be to God who gives victory to the followers of the Mahomedian Faith.

Praise be to His Prophet Mahomed whose religion is glorious; to the Prophets, apostles, and descendants whose dignities are very high, and also to all the believers of the Mahomedan Faith, and to the Ghazies who are exalted.

O Brethren! At this present time, the execrable Christians are openly committing oppression and tyranny; they are killing innocent men, plundering their property, setting fire to their houses and shutting up their children in houses, some of which they burn down and the doors of others they build up (sic). It has been very difficult for the *Hafezes,* the learned and the pious to live in their houses. The said Christians felt no hesitation whatever in hanging great chiefs. These accursed Christians are so ungodly and inhuman, that they forcibly press many poor people into their service, tie the hands of one with those of another (leaving no gap at all between the

6

ribs and the hands), in the form of a *Tuttee* or shutter and then, by pricking them with bayonets, force them to go in front to the field of battle, using them as shields for their own defence, while they themselves follow these helpless ones under the shelter of their bodies, which in consequence, are struck by shots etc. Such has been the state of anarchy that the whole country has been insecure and plunderers are robbing the villagers and travellers with impunity while they (the Christians) are unemployed. They are also hanging men and ravaging villages. In fact these outrageous acts are a prelude to the downfall of this (sic) accursed people. As their past conduct in attempting to deprive the troops of their religion, by applying impure substances to the cartridges and pressing those troops to use them, led to their destruction like dogs, as well as to the loss of their army and territories; so their present proceedings have converted their subjects also into their enemies.

This (sic) accursed people have considered themselves as equal to the great Pharoah, but they will all, please God, be butchered in the same manner as Pharoah. If they succeed in re-establishing their authority, *great misfortunes will befall all the Hindoos and Mahomedans*, the people, the sepoys, the Kings and the *Wuzeers*. The delay in the annihilation of these Christians is involving the loss of many innocent lives, a circumstance which renders the waging of a religious war at once with the execrable Christians one of our bounden duties, enjoined by the Prophet. God be praised that the necessary material for the execution of that duty has through his assistance been now put in our possession i.e., the guns etc., which are required for a religious war and which formerly the people of Hindoostan stood in need of;

these are through the Divine favour now in the possession of the Mahomedan Kings of Delhi, and Lucknow. May God save the Kings of the Mahomedans and make them victorious. A few troops of the English are still alive, but they are paralyzed. Whoever will not take advantage of this opportunity to make a religious war, will repent in future as such a chance will never again offer.

Consider that formerly it was not in the power of even the Nawabs and the Rajas to kill even a common sepoy of the British, but now shoemakers and sellers of spirituous liquors have destroyed British gentlemen of high dignity. As the sepoys first commenced killing them who in who, in retaliation, are spilling the blood of innocent men and desolation their houses, they (the sepoys) should now proceed to every country and city and put the Christians to death that they (the sepoys) may not be held responsible on the day of Judgment, for their former acts. The sepoys ought not to assemble, all at one place, since the execrable English go everywhere, and fight. Though they are a low people like the shoemakers and spirit sellers, and have but a small body of troops, yet they get intelligence from every place. They wish by deceit to induce you to shut yourselves up in one place, so that you may be unable to go forward. For this purpose a small number of Europeans make their appearance at any place with toys in their hands, or having vermillion applied to some member of their bodies in order that you may imagine that they are about to practise enchantment on you, but in reality they come to deceive you, and their object in making their appearance in this manner is not to practise enchantment on you. Even if it be taken for granted that their object is enchantment, still it cannot avail them, as it becomes defeated by the repetition of the invocation 'Allah-Akber'. They sometimes give out that Europeans have arrived at certain places and through this craft (which is like that of a fox) confound the people; you should not, however, be confounded, but speak this, 'If they are come, what it matters? They will all be destroyed.' You ought to press on to such places as Cawnpore etc. What difficulty is there in going to Cawnpore? If you dread the mud fort of Cawnpore, whom have you chosen to reduce the Forts of Allahabad and Calcutta? It is you sepoys who have kindled the flames and these cannot be extinguished but by you. You should therefore fight and pray. Do not put off till tomorrow that which can be done today, and whatever it is possible to do today, let it be done forthwith. It is now incumbent on the sepoys to consider the protection of Delhi and Lucknow as their first care, inasmuch as *these two places are the asylums of the sepoys and the people high and low,* and the Enemies have fixed their teeth on them, but God has made a bitter morsel for their teeth, and will continue to do so. A sufficient number of sepoys should be stationed in these two cities to protect them and to construct batteries at 8 or 10 miles distance from them in every direction. The remaining sepoys, after receiving orders from the King, should proceed to the East being accompanied by the fanatics [This word, obviously, has been used for Ghazis.] who desire to make a religious war. They should kill and pursue the unbelieving people as far as Calcutta, congregating together in the same manner as clouds overspread the sky in the Turkish Empire and Syria. By doing so, Delhi and Lucknow will be well protected. It is above all things a duty to collect the people desirous of waging a religious war. There is no necessity for writing the advantages which will be derived from assembling them, since they are well known, and are of such importance as to be well worthy of the attention of the Ruler of the Country. If the Troops do not proceed to the East, the result will not be good. The advantages which will result need not be described, as they are manifest. Arise quickly in the name of God, and go forth to slay the infidels. May the Almighty give you strength, courage and victory. *Cause it to be proclaimed by beat of drum, that the sepoys are prohibited from plundering any one, more especially the people of the places which they may conquer.* The enemies have plundered those for whose protection you are going. If you also plunder them, to whom will they look for protection? *Punish immediately the plunderer and cause the plundered property to be restored to its owner. Pillage is the part of a criminal.* It is unlawful to say prayers, keeping the bier of such a person in the front for the benefit of his soul. *It is however lawful to plunder the property of the enemy; such plundered property is designated 'Prize'.*

The Chief (under whose command you will achieve conquests) will explain to you how that prize is to be divided among you. The persons whose property is plundered, curse the plunderers and their maledictions become quickly efficacious. The Prophet has said that the prayers of oppressed people are immediately granted by God. It is only through the efficacy of the maledictions of these men, that you have recently succeeded in killing the English of high dignity and thousands of Europeans; but, you are now flying before a small body of Europeans, whom even the shoemakers and spirit-sellers can put to death. Do not destroy any one else, but those with whom you may be at war. A man with whom you are not fighting ought to be put to death for his crimes by the executioner under orders of the King. It is the part of the sepoys and Religious fanatics, to destroy the infidels in the field of battle. The people should at present, offer thanks to the Almighty, and fight valorously, because this is the way to make good provisions for themselves. In the time of the Prophet (Mahomed) one thousand Mahomedans, living on the leaves of trees, fought with eighty thousand infidels. It is stated in the Koran that one hundred pious Mahomedans can, by the power of God, overcome two hundred infidels and in like manner one thousand Mahomedans can overcome two thousand infidels. This blessing can be obtained if a holy leader be first appointed and then a religious war be undertaken. Now unite together, invoking God, and become of one mind. If you do not find a Koreshee at the time when the infidels are paramount in power, it is of no consequence. Appoint a Mahomedan who is a Chief and in power, to be the leader of the Mahomedans and solemnly declare yourselves as his followers in order that his orders may have weight and force amongst you and others, so that all doubts may be removed and that your hearts may be fixed on killing the enemy or on dying yourselves. These arrangements will of course afford every satisfaction to us all.

It is incumbent on one thousand *Ghazees* to be steadfast in opposing two thousand infidels, but it is unlawful for them to take flight. The more obstinately they will fight, the greater spiritual benefit will accrue to them. Hence, the Ghazees, though one thousand in number, will please God, never fly even before ten thousand Europeans.

Kursh is an animal living in the sea, all other creatures of which dread it. From this word the term 'Koresh' above alluded to has been derived. Koresh means little Kursh, the letter 'e' being added to it. Ghaleb, son of Taher, who was one of the ancestors of the last Prophet, was called 'Koresh' on the ground that all the nations dreaded him. His descendants are designated Koreshees. The Syuds, Siddikies, Furookies, Osmanees, Alvees and the Abbassee Sheiks are Koreshees. The Arabs are the bravest of all the nations in the whole world and the Koreshees are the most courageous amongst the Arabs. Hence God made the last Prophet a descendant of the Koreshee family of Arabia and caused the Koreshees and all other Arabs to be his descendants and the followers of his faith, in order that when the Arabians and Koreshees should be zealous for their religion, such religion might be propagated throughout the world. Certain sages have therefore pronounced it unlawful to appoint Commanders except of the Koreshee family. But if at the time when the infidels become paramount in power, a Koreshee be not found, any Mahomedan Chief endowed even with a few of the qualities of a leader and observing the tenets of the Mahomedan Law can, as a matter of necessity, be selected as Chief. This leader will be called *Imam Akher* and great benefits will be derived from him in the cause of our faith. The leader who draws money on pretence of fighting for the faith, and appropriates it in his own use, is a great hypocrite. In short it is held lawful, even by the religious books, that the orders of a Mahomedian Chief, of whatever description he may be, should be obeyed. *Common sense and a regard for faith point out that servitude under the Mahomedan Chiefs and such Rajahs as are dependants of the Mahomedan Kings is infinitely better than that, under the infidel Victoria and the English,* the enemies of our faith. After a Chief has been appointed, he will select other Chiefs among the army, some of whom will command the Pioneers, (or the persons who lie in an ambuscade in the day time and make attacks at night and who do not exceed four thousand in number nor fall short of four hundred and sometimes whose least number is 100) and others will lead the *Jaesh,* whose number is unlimited, but does not fall short of four thousand. The leaders of these two classes are called *Ameer Serrya* and *Ameer Jaesh* respectively. It is our bounden duty to obey the command of these two grades of leaders, agreeably to the orders of the Chief Commander as also to serve the latter.

The Hindoos should join the Chief with a view to defend their religion, and should solemnly pledge themselves (to be faithful); the Hindoos and the Mahomedans, as brethren to each other, should also butcher the English, inasmuch as formerly the Mahomedan Kings protected (as they felt it incumbent on them to do) the lives and property of the Hindoos with their children in the same manner as protected those of the Mahomedans, and all the Hindoos with heart and soul were obedient and loyal to the Mahomedan Kings. The very Hindoos and Mahomedan Nations with the very books are not existing. *The Hindoos will remain steadfast to their religion, while we will also retain ours.* Aid and protection will be offered by us to each other. The accursed Christians were anxious to make both the Hindoos and the Mahomedans, Christians, but, by God's blessing they themselves have, on the contrary, been ruined. They have now no troops, not even in England. All have been destroyed, with the exception of a small number in this country. They should be annihilated and thereby all the disturbances will be at an end. The adoption of the following measures will lead to their destruction, viz.: A proclamation should be issued both to the troops and people of Bengal if possible, or if otherwise, as far as possible at present, to the effect that the people of every city, whether Hindoos or Mahomedans, should be unanimous in attaching simultaneously this accursed nation (by the appointment of a leader in each city). *If all the attack be made in one and the same day, it will be well and good, if otherwise, they ought to be made in one and the same month, but at an interval of 2 or 4 days, only in order, that these execrable men may see no hope whatever, in assembling themselves at any city, but may remain, in small at different places and thus be destroyed.* Our object in repeatedly requiring you to appoint Chiefs, is to gain for you the spiritual benefit and speedy mercy of God, from the execution of the injunctions of the Mahomedan Law, and not to remain without a Chief. The fact is that the English have a Chief over them, but not God in their favour; whereas He sides with us. He has provided us, the Mahomedans, with a King to arrange our affairs, but as our arrangements are lately made, whereas those of the English are of a century's standing, and as disturbances have taken place everywhere, how is it then possible for one individual (the King) to be present at every place or to depute Chiefs there, since he has no time to do so? It is therefore incumbent on us to appoint a leader or Chief forthwith and to obey his commands for the purpose of destroying the English. The adoption of the following measures will lead to their destruction, viz.: the Ghazees, among the people as well as those among the troops, both horse and foot, who are very brave and experienced in War, should with one accord slay the Christians in the field of battle, invoking at the same time *Allah Akber*. The people should seek opportunities to harass the enemy and render every service to the sepoys who should employ all the skill they have acquired in killing the English and should take example from the acts of the latter, i.e., if the English sit down, they should lie down; if the English divide their Army into three or more parts, our sepoys should make as many divisions of the troops or more than those divisions, and two or three division of theirs. Besides this they should act up to the established rules. They should fire such guns of such calibre, that their balls may scatter the English on the ground, while those of the latter may not reach them. They are to surround the English by stratagem and kill them. They are in like manner either, to destroy the houses in which Christians may have concealed themselves or to make a breach for their entrance therein by firing guns of such large calibre as can dismantle a fort. When fire is to be opened, it is to be kept up so briskly that the enemy may not have time to return it. Several guns are to be fired at once, at the time, when they may be expected to do much execution. The Artillery men are to take the usual rest, but the fire is to be kept up. If they have to fight for three hours, they should keep with them a sufficient quantity of ammunition to last them for 24 hours. They should make a simultaneous attack and not allow their men to be slain by dividing them into small bodies. If they make simultaneous attack all the infidels will be paralyzed, through fear of a large body of troops and be destroyed. It is enjoined by our faith that all its ordinances should be observed at the times appointed for their execution. When it does not rain, man is obliged to go out to the meadow to pray to the Almighty for rain. The time has now come for the appointment of a leader to wage a religious war. When a leader is to be appointed, all misfortunes will be at an end and a report of the commencement of a religious war will be spread. The Ghazees will come from every direction and your troops will be innumerable as locusts.

It is a fact, that the solemn promise of sepoy to his commander on the occasion of a religious war is as binding as that of a person to his Spiritual Guide, at the time of the expiation of his sins. The fulfilment of such solemn act by anyone wins for him great advantages and blessings and makes him always successful. When a man makes such solemn declaration to his Spiritual Guide, he feels that he will derive spiritual benefit from him; he entertains strong feelings of attachment and devotion towards him; he looks upon all his acts as correct and good and he considers it easy under his orders to sacrifice his life, property, and honour in the path to God. In like manner the sepoys in obeying the orders of their commander (who is regarded as a Spiritual Guide) will, with readiness devote their lives to the service of the Almighty. When there is already a Chief in power in any city it is unnecessary to seek for another Chief to make him a leader, for the Almighty has already provided that place with a Chief and it is unlawful to appoint two leaders at one and the same place, a law which is prescribed in the Theological Books. It is incumbent on the people to appoint that Chief as their commander and to act up to his order and to consider him as their Spiritual Guide and also with one accord under his command to butcher all the Europeans. They (the sepoys) should, with heart and soul, render obedience to their immediate commandant, whom the commander will appoint and should expel the English infidels from this Country as early as possible. The *Ameer* of the *Jaesh* (i.e., the Commander-in-Chief) will be present with them and issue commands to the right and left wings of the Army as he may deem necessary. He will skilfully lead the troops. When the leader is not skilled in war, he suffers defeat. A good General obtains victory by a skilful disposition of his forces. We give as a specimen the following rules of warfare. The other rules are well known to the brave sepoys, viz. in the first place count the number of fighting men and prepare muster rolls; appoint intelligent and faithful men as your spies, that they may furnish news not only every day and night, but hourly, regarding the army of the enemy, since spies are the hands and legs of the person who employs them. The accursed English have been saved from destruction only by the help of spies. When a body of troops are doing battle at any place, all other troops should render them every assistance, even though not previously acquainted with them. For they ought to know, that the disgrace of a defeat of the troops engaged in war, will not be confined to them alone, but that on the contrary, the discomfiture of any troops in India will expose all the people thereof to shame. When they hear of the attack of an enemy, they should hold consultation with all the troops and occupy themselves day and night in taking steps to expel the enemy. After the consultation has been held, they should select one thousand or five hundred of the strongest youths (more or less, as circumstances require), fit for making an attack unawares. These should hide themselves in a neighbouring place, and on receiving correct information from their spies, they should attack the enemy all of a sudden when they find them negligent and careless. They should apply themselves to the execution of the duties which have been already appointed (sic, assigned) to them. Some of them should cut the ropes of the tents, others should severe the heel ropes and hind stalls of the horses. Some should seize upon the arms and guns, others should fire volleys on the enemy, and put them to the sword. Some should hide themselves in the jungles, ravines, and valleys, and cut off the supplies of the enemy and kill, both in the day time and at night, their *Syees* (grass-cutters), horse and foot and also their spies. They should continue to do so through a vast tract of land, extending many miles. They should make satisfactory arrangements regarding the rivers. The enemy will, please God, be driven even from the most distant places.

When the troops have to fight in the open plain, they should first hold a deliberate consultation evincing resignation to the Almighty and they should offer up fervent prayers to him. All the Hindoos and Mahomedans will afterwards invoke God and commence fighting. It is lawful to attack unawares and deceive an enemy so that stratagems should be resorted to but mutual promises should not be broken. All should be unanimous and vigilant in the field of the battle. The Commanders and Chiefs should encourage the Troops, and incite them by shouts, exclaiming thus, 'Oh Warriors brave', 'Oh Warriors, you have fought desperately'. 'Oh Warriors, you have overcome the enemy'. 'Oh Warriors, why should it not be so?' 'A hundred thanks are due to your mother, whose mil has proved so invigorating.' 'Oh Warriors, now the victory is gained.' 'Advance Warriors.' 'Advance Brethren.' 'Advance Heroes, we have not gained the victory.' 'Be bolder my Warriors, we have now gained the victory. Behold the enemy are turning their backs.' 'Good! Oh my Warriors, and strike.' 'Oh my tiger tigers, pounce upon the Jackals.' 'Bravo! Brave.' 'Oh Brethren, you have saved my nose today.' 'Bravo! Brave.'

'Oh Ghazees, you have upheld my honour.' 'Oh Warriors, take care that you do not incur the shame of losing this turban.' 'Oh Ghazees, be careful, lest you incur shame, if I lose by beard.' 'Oh Brethren, kill the enemy.' 'Oh Warriors, slay the enemy.' 'Oh Ghazees, I have sacrificed my parents to you.' Sometimes the Commanders and Chiefs should taunt the enemy in the manner: 'Why? Oh ye noxious ones, Whither are your flying now?' 'Why? Oh ye noxious ones, you are now fighting with Tigers.' 'Why? Oh ye eaters of forbidden things, are you not now under the influence of liquor?' 'Why? Oh cowards, have you now forgotten manoeuvres? Why are you running away? Are the swords now brandished?' and so on.

Now hear a proclamation which will answer our purpose.

PROCLAMATION

Before the quarrel regarding the cartridges took place, these accursed English had written to the Impure Victoria thus: 'If Your Majesty will permit us to kill 15 *Moulvees* out of every hundred in India and the same number out of every hundred *Pundits,* as well as five hundred thousand of Hindoos and Mahomedan sepoys and *Ryuts,* we will in a short time make all the people of India "Christian".' Then that ill-starred, polluted Bitch gave her consent to the spilling of this innocent blood. She did not reflect at all that she was not at liberty to permit the commission of the murder of the creatures of God. The accursed men, on the receipt of her permission, commenced committing general slaughter on the pretext of the cartridges. As no one was in a condition to oppose them, they would in a short time have killed every one who refused to become a Christian, had it not been that, by God's blessings, the bold sepoys butchered the English and put an end to all their power. They have weakened them in such a degree that it has been easy to kill or expel them. If the daring sepoys put the remainder of their enemies to death, and if all the people be engaged in taking steps for their destruction and if none of the Hindoos and Mahomedans will serve them in any way, and if they consider that as a consequence of serving the English, they will be regarded as accomplices in the commission of the murder of the Pundits and Moulvees and also if all the people unite in killing them, it will then be well and good; otherwise it will not be so. It has become the bounden duty of all the people whether women or men, slave girls or slaves, to come forward and put the English to death. The adoption of the following measures will lead to their destruction, viz.: all the Moulvees and the Pundits should explain in every village and city the misfortunes which the success of the English will entail on the people and the advantages and spiritual benefit which will accrue from their extirpation. The Kings, Wuzeers, Rajahs and Nawabs ought to slay them in the field of battle, the people should not leave their city in consequence of the entrance of the English therein, but on the contrary should shut up their doors and all the people whether men, women or children, including slave girls, slaves, and old women, ought to put these accursed English to death by firing guns, carbines and pistols, bricks, earthen vessels, ladles, old shoes and all other things, which may come into their hands. They should stone to death the English in the same manner as the swallows stoned the Chief of the elephants. The sepoys, the nobles, the shopkeepers, the oil men, etc. and all other people of the city, being of one accord, should make a simultaneous attack upon them, some of them should kill them by firing guns, pistols, and carbines and with swords, arrows, daggers, poignando, etc., some lift them up on spears, some dexterously snatch their arms and destroy the enemy, some should cling to their necks, some to their waists, some should wrestle and through stratagem break the enemy to pieces; some attack them with their fists, some scratch them, some drag them along, some tear out their ears, some break their noses. In short no one should spare any efforts to destroy the enemy and reduce them to the greatest extremities. Under such circumstances they will be unable to do anything, though they may amount to lakhs of men. They will all, please God, be put to death. It is necessary to make this Proclamation generally known.

APPENDIX D TO CHAPTER 3

PROCLAMATION OF BAHADUR SHAH
(25 AUGUST 1857)

It is well known to all that in this age the people of Hindoostan, both Hindoos and Mohammedans, are being ruined under the tyranny and oppression of the infidel and treacherous English. It is therefore the bounden duty of all the wealthy people of India, especially of those who have any sort of connection with any of the Mohammedan royal families, and are considered the pastors and masters of their people, to stake their lives and property for the wellbeing of the public. With the view of effecting this general good, several princes belonging to the royal family of Delhi have dispersed themselves in the different parts of India, Iran, Turan, and Afghanistan, and have been long since taking measures to compass their favourite end; and it is to accomplish this charitable object that one of the aforesaid princes has, at the head of an army of Afghanistan, &c., made his appearance in India; and I, who am the grandson of Abul Muzuffer Serajuddin Bahadur Shah Ghazee, King of India, having in the course of circuit come here to extirpate the infidels residing in the eastern part of the country, and to liberate and protect the poor helpless people now groaning under their iron rule have, by the aid of the *Majahdees,* or religious fanatics erected the standard of Mohammed, and persuaded the orthodox Hindoos who had been subject to my ancestors, and have been and are still accessories in the destruction of the English, to raise the standard of Mahavir.

Several of the Hindoos and Mussalman chiefs, who have long since quitted their homes for the preservation of their religion, and have been trying their best to root out the English in India, have presented themselves to me, and taken part in the reigning Indian crusade, and it is more than probable that I shall very shortly receive succours from the West. Therefore, for the information of the public, the present Ishtahar, consisting of several sections, is put in circulation, and it is the imperative duty of all to take it into their careful consideration, and abide by it. Parties anxious to participate in the common cause, but having no means to provide for themselves, shall receive their daily subsistence from me; and be it known to all, that the ancient works, both of the Hindoos and the Mohammedans, the writings of the miracle workers, and the calculations of the astrologers, pundits, and rammals, all agree in asserting that the English will no longer have any footing in India or elsewhere. Therefore it is incumbent on all to give up the hope of the continuation of the British sway side with me, and deserve the consideration of the Badshahi, or imperial Government, by their individual exertion in promoting the common good, and thus attain their respective ends; otherwise if this golden opportunity slips away, they will have to repent of their folly, as it is very aptly said by a poet in two fine couplets, the drift whereof is 'Never let a favourable opportunity slip, for in the field of opportunity you are to meet with the ball of fortune; but if you do not avail yourself of the opportunity that offers itself, you will have to bite your finger through grief.

No person, at the misrepresentation of the well-wishers of the British Government, ought to conclude from the present slight inconveniences usually attendant on revolutions, that similar inconveniences and troubles should continue when the Badshahi Government is established on a firm basis; and parties badly dealt with by any sepoy or plunderer, should come up and represent their grievances to me, and receive redress at my hands; and for whatever property they may lose in the reigning disorder, they will be recompensed from the public treasury when the Badshahi Government is well fixed.

Section I—Regarding Zemindars—It is evident, that the British Government in making zemindary settlements have imposed exorbitant *Jumas*, and have disgraced and ruined several zemindars, by putting up their estates to public auction for arrears of rent, in so much as, that on the institution of a suit by a common Ryot, a maid servant or a slave, the respectable zemindars are summoned into courts, arrested, put in gaol and disgraced. In litigations regarding zemindaries, the immense value of stamps, and other unnecessary expenses of the civil courts, which are pregnant with all sorts of crooked dealings, and the practice of allowing a case to hang on for years, are all calculated to impoverish the litigants. Besides this, the coffers of the zemindars are annually taxed with subscription for schools, hospitals, roads etc. Such extortions will have no manner of existence in the Badshahi Government; but, on the contrary, the Jumas will be light, the dignity and honour of the zemindars safe, and every zemindari will have absolute rule in his own zemindary. The zemindary disputes will be summarily decided according to the Shurrah and the Shasters, without any expense; and the zemindars who will assist in the present war with their men and money, shall be excused for ever from paying half the revenue. Zemindars aiding only with money, shall be excepted in perpetuity from paying one-fourth of the revenue and should any zemindari who has been unjustly deprived of his lands during the English Government, personally join the war, he will be restored to his Zemindary, and excused from paying one-fourth of the revenue.

Section II—Regarding Merchants—It is plain that the infidel and treacherous British Government have monopolized the trade of all the fine and valuable merchandise, such as indigo, cloth, and other articles of shipping, leaving only the trade of trifles to the people, and even in this they are not without their share of the profits, which they secure by means of customs and stamp fees, &c. in money suits, so that the people have merely a trade in name. Besides this, the profits of the traders are taxed, with postages, tolls, and subscriptions for schools, &c. Notwithstanding all these concessions, the merchants are liable to imprisonment and disgrace at the instance or complaint of a worthless man. When the Badshahi Government is established, all these aforesaid fraudulent practices shall be dispensed with, and the trade of every article, without exception, both by land and water, shall be open to the native merchants of India, who will have the benefit of the Government steam-vessels and steam-carriages for the conveyance of their merchandise gratis; and merchants having no capital of their own shall be assisted from the public treasury. It is therefore the duty of every merchant to take part in the war, and aid the Badshahi Government with his men and money, either secretly or openly, as may be consistent with his position or interest, and forswear his allegiance to the British Government.

Section III—Regarding Public Servants—It is not a secret thing, that under the British Government, natives employed in the civil and military services, have little respect, low pay, and no manner of influence; and all the posts of dignity and emoluments in both the departments, are exclusively bestowed on Englishmen for natives in the military service, after having devoted the greater part of their lives, attain to the post of soobadar (the very height of their hopes) with a salary of 60r. or 70r. per mensem; and those in the civil service obtain the post of Sudder Ala, with a salary of 500 r. a month, but no influence, jagheer, or present. But under the Badshahi Government like the posts of colonel, general, and commander-in-chief, which the English enjoy at present, the corresponding posts of Pansadi, Punj-hazari, Haft-hazari, and Sippah-salari, will be given to the natives in the military service; and, like the post of collector, magistrate, judge, sudder judge, secretary and governor, which the European civil servants now hold, the corresponding posts of Wuzeer, Quazi, Safir, Suba Nizam (Nazim) and Dewan, &c., with salaries of Lacs of Rupees, will be given to the natives of the civil service, together with jagheers, khilluts, inams, and influence. Natives, whether Hindoos or Mohammedans, who fall fighting against the English, are sure to go to heaven; and those killed fighting for the English, will doubtless, go to hell. Therefore, all the natives in the British service ought to be alive to their religion and interest, and abjuring their loyalty to the English, side with the Badshahi Government, and obtain salaries of 200 or 300 rupees per month for the present, and be entitled to high posts in future. If they, for any reason, cannot at present declare openly against the English, they can heartily wish ill to their cause, and remain passive spectators of passing events, without taking any active share therein. But at the same time they should indirectly assist the Badshahi Government, and try their best to drive the English out of the country.

All the sepoys and sowars who have, for the sake of their religion, joined in the destruction of the English, and are at present, on any consideration, in a state of concealment, either at home or elsewhere, should present themselves to me without the least delay or hesitation.

Foot soldiers will be paid at the rate of three annas, and sowars at eight or twelve annas per diem for the present, and afterwards they will be paid double of what they get in the British service. Soldiers not in the English service, and taking part in the war against the English, will receive their daily subsistence money according to the rates specified below for the present; and in future the foot soldiers will be paid at the rate of eight or ten rupees, and sowars at the rate of twenty or thirty rupees, per month; and on the permanent establishment of the Badshahi Government, will stand entitled to the highest post in the state, to jagheers and presents :-

Matchlockmen	...	2 annas a day
Riflemen	...	2 ½ annas a day
Swordsmen	...	1 ½ annas a day
Horsemen, with large horses	...	8 annas a day
Horsemen, with small horses	...	6 annas a day

Section IV—Regarding Artisans—It is evident that the Europeans, by the introduction of English articles into India, have thrown the weavers, the cotton dressers, the carpenters, the blacksmiths, and the shoemakers, &c., out of employ, and have engrossed their occupations, so that every description of native artisan has been reduced to beggary. But under the Badshahi Government the native artisans will exclusively be employed in the services of the kings, the rajahs, and the rich; and this will no doubt ensure their prosperity. Therefore these artisans ought to renounce the English services, and assist the Majahdeens, or religious fanatics, engaged in the war, and thus be entitled both to secular and eternal happiness.

Section V—Regarding Pundits, Fakirs and other learned persons—The pundits and fakirs being the guardians of the Hindoo and Mohammedan religions respectively, and the Europeans being the enemies of both the religions, and as at present a war is raging against the English on account of religion, the pundits and fakirs are bound to present themselves to me, and take this share in the holy war, otherwise they will stand condemned according to the tenor of the Shurrah and the Shasters; but if they come, they will, when the Badshahi Government is well established, receive rent-free lands.

Lastly, be it known to all, that whoever, out of the above names, classes, shall after the circulation of this Ishtahar, still cling to the British Government, all his estates shall be confiscated, and his property plundered, and he himself, with his whole family, shall be imprisoned, and ultimately put to death.

ACKNOWLEDGEMENTS

This is a lockdown book: it was written entirely when I was housebound. Fortunately, I had finished the archival research for this book before the lockdown. But even then, the book could not have been written without access to secondary material. I could have this access thanks to the unfailing courtesy of three remarkable gentlemen: Saktidas Roy of the Anandabazar Patrika library, who in my twenty-five years of my knowing him has never failed to deliver on a request; and B.P. Prakash and Bibhutinath Jha of the Ashoka University library, who, working under very trying and challenging circumstances, provided me with all the books and articles I asked for. Without the kindness of these three persons, this book would never have been written.

Partha Chatterjee read and offered comments on parts of the typescript. Saleem Kidwai, who embodies the grace and the learning of a Lucknow long past and long forgotten, also read sections of the book. Ishan Chauhan provided help regarding his great grandmother, Subhadra Kumari Chauhan, the author of that memorable poem on the Rani of Jhansi. Rukun Advani cast his editorial eye on the entire typescript.

I cherish his friendship and value the care with which he corrects the infelicities of my English prose.

Every time I write a book on the revolt of 1857, I tell myself that it is the last one on the subject. I cannot promise readers that this is the last time I will inflict on them my ruminations on the rebellion. I am not at all sure if I chase the revolt or it chases me!

BIBLIOGRAPHY

I. ARCHIVAL SOURCES

British Library, London, India Office Records
Board's Collection
Home Miscellaneous
North Western Provinces Political Proceedings
Collections to Political Despatches
Political and Secret Department
National Archives of India, New Delhi
Foreign Department, Secret Consultations
Foreign Department, Political Consultations
Foreign Department, Political Proceedings
Foreign Department, Secret Proceedings

II. PRINTED SOURCES

Forrest, G.W., *Selections from Letters, Despatches and State Papers in the Military Department of the Government of India, 1857–58*, 4 vols (Calcutta: Government of India: 1893–1912).

Papers Relating to Indian Mutinies, 3 vols (London: 1857).

III. SECONDARY WORKS: BOOKS AND ARTICLES

Arnold, E., *The Marquess of Dalhousie's Administration of British India*, 2 vols (London: Saunders, Otley & Co.: 1865).

Baird, J.G.A., *Private Letters of the Marquess of Dalhousie* (Edinburgh: W. Blackwood and Sons: 1910).

Ball, Charles, *The History of the Indian Mutiny* (London: London Printing & Publishing Company: n.d.).

Barat, A., *The Bengal Native Infantry: Its Organization and Discipline, 1796–1852* (Calcutta: Firma K.L. Mukhopadhyay: 1962).

Barnett, R.B., *North India Between Empires: Awadh, the Mughals and the British, 1720–1801* (Berkeley: University of California Press: 1980).

Basu, P., *Oudh and the English East India Company, 1785–1801* (Lucknow: Maxwell Company: 1943).

Bayly, C.A., *Empire and Information: Intelligence Gathering and Social Communication in India, 1780–1870* (Cambridge: Cambridge University Press: 1996).

Bayly, C.A., *Origins of Nationality in South Asia: Patriotism and Ethical Government in the Making of Modern India* (Delhi: Oxford University Press: 1998).

Bayly, C.A., *Rulers, Townsmen and Bazaars: North Indian Society in the Age of British Expansion, 1770–1870* (Cambridge: Cambridge University Press: 1983).

Bhadra, Gautam, 'Four Rebels of 1857' in R. Guha (ed.) *Subaltern Studies: Writings on South Asian History and Society*, vol. IV (Delhi: Oxford University Press: 1986).

Bhatnagar, G.D., 'The Annexation of Oudh', *Uttara Bharati*, vol. 3 (1956).

Chakrabarty, Dipesh, *The Calling of History: Sir Jadunath Sarkar and His Empire of Truth* (Ranikhet: Permanent Black and Ashoka University: 2015).

Chandra, Satish, *Parties and Politics in the Mughal Court 1707–1740* (Aligarh: Aligarh Muslim University: 1959; repr. Delhi: People's Publishing House: 1972).

Chatterjee, Partha, *Nationalist Thought and the Colonial World: A Derivative Discourse?* (London: Zed Press: 1986).

Chatterjee, Partha, *The Nation and its Fragments: Colonial and Postcolonial Histories* (Delhi: Oxford University Press: 1994).

Chaudhuri, S.B., *Civil Rebellion in the Indian Mutinies: 1857–1859* (Calcutta: The World Press: 1957).

Chaudhuri, S.B., *English Historical Writings on the Indian Mutiny, 1857–1859* (Calcutta: The World Press: 1979).

Crooke, W., 'Songs about the King of Oudh', *Indian Antiquary*, vol. XL, 1911.

Dalrymple, William, *The Last Mughal: The Fall of a Dynasty, Delhi, 1857* (Delhi: Bloomsbury: 2006).

David, Saul, *The Indian Mutiny, 1857* (London: Viking: 2002).

Deshpande, Prachi, 'The Making of an Indian Nationalist Archive: Lakshmibai, Jhansi and 1857' in *Journal of Asian Studies*, vol. 67, No. 3 (August 2008).

Dundas Robertson, H., *District Duties During the Revolt in the North-West Provinces of India in 1857: With Subsequent Investigations During 1858–59* (London: Smith, Elder: 1859).

Dunlop, R.H.W., *Service and Adventure with the Khakee Ressalah or Meerut Volunteer Horse, During the Mutinies of 1857–58* (London: Richard Bentley: 1858).

Edwardes, H.B., and Merivale, H., *Life of Sir Henry Lawrence*, 2 vols (London: Smith Elder: 1873).

Edwards, W., *Personal Adventures During the Indian Rebellion in Rohilkhand, Futtehghur and Oude* (London: Smith Elder & Co: 1858).

Godse, Vishnu Bhatt, *1857: The Real Story of the Great Uprising* translated by Mrinal Pande (New Delhi: Harper Perennial: 2011).

Gubbins, M., *An Account of the Mutinies in Oude and the Siege of the Lucknow Residency* (London: Richard Bentley: 1858).

Guha, Ranajit, *Elementary Aspects of Peasant Insurgency in Colonial India* (Delhi: Oxford University Press: 1983).

Guha, Ranajit, 'The Prose of Counter Insurgency' in R. Guha (ed.) *Subaltern Studies: Writings on South Asian History and Society*, vol. 2 (Delhi: Oxford University Press: 1983).

Guha, Ranajit, *Dominance without Hegemony: History and Power in Colonial India* (Delhi: Oxford University Press: 1998).

Guha, Sumit, *History and Collective Memory in South Asia, 1200–2000* (Ranikhet: Permanent Black and Ashoka University: 2019).

Hibbert, C., *The Great Mutiny: India, 1857* (Penguin: Harmondsworth: 1978).

Joshi, P.C., *Rebellion, 1857: A Symposium* (Delhi: People's Publishing House: 1957; repr., Calcutta: K.P. Bagchi: 1986).

Kaye, J.W., *History of the Sepoy War*, 3 vols (London: W.H. Allen: 1864–76).

Lal, Ruby, *Coming of Age in Nineteenth-Century India: The Girl Child and the Art of Playfulness* (Cambridge: Cambridge University Press: 2013).

Llewellyn-Jones, Rosie (ed.), *The Uprising of 1857* (Ahmedabad: Alkazi Collection of Photography and Mappin: 2017).

MacLagan, M., *Clemency Canning* (London: Macmillan: 1962).

Majumdar, R.C., *The Sepoy Mutiny and the Revolt of 1857* (Calcutta: Firma K.L. Mukhopadhyay: 1957).

Malleson, G.B., *A History of the Indian Mutiny*, 3 vols (London: Longmans Green & Company: 1878–80).

Marshall, Peter, 'Economic and Political Expansion: The Case of Oudh', *Modern Asian Studies*, vol. 9, No. 4 (1975).

Marx, K. & Engels, F., *The First War of Indian Independence* (Moscow: Progress Publishers: 1967 repr.).

Metcalf, T.R., *The Aftermath of Revolt: India, 1857–70* (Princeton: Princeton University Press: 1964).

Metcalf, T.R., *Land, Landlords and the British Raj: Northern India in the Nineteenth Century* (Berkeley: University of California Press: 1979).

Mukherjee, Rudrangshu, *Awadh in Revolt, 1857–58: A Study of Popular Resistance* (Delhi: Oxford University Press; 1984; repr. Ranikhet: Permanent Black: 2001; repr. Ranikhet: Permanent Black and Ashoka University: 2019).

Mukherjee, Rudrangshu, *Spectre of Violence: The 1857 Kanpur Massacres* (Delhi: Penguin: 1998; repr. 2007).

Mukherjee, Rudrangshu, *Mangal Pandey: Brave Martyr or Accidental Hero?* (Delhi: Penguin: 2005).

Mukherjee, Rudrangshu, *1857: Revolt Against the Raj* (Delhi: Roli: 2008).

Mukherjee, Rudrangshu, *The Year of Blood: Essays on 1857* (Delhi: Social Science Press: 2014).

Mukherjee, Rudrangshu, 'Trade and Empire in Awadh, 1765–1804, *Past and Present*, No. 94, Feb. 1982.

Mukherjee, Rudrangshu and Marshall, Peter, 'Debate: Early British Imperialism in India', in *Past and Present*, No. 106, February 1985.

Nehru, Jawaharlal, *An Autobiography* (London: The Bodley Head: 1936).

Nehru, Jawaharlal, *The Discovery of India* (Calcutta: Signet Press: 1946).

Palmer, J.A.B., *The Mutiny Outbreak at Meerut in 1857* (Cambridge: Cambridge University Press: 1966).

Pandey, Gyanendra, *A History of Prejudice: Race, Caste, and Difference in India and the United States* (Cambridge: University Press: 2013).

Pemble, J., *The Raj, the Indian Mutiny and the Kingdom of Oudh* (Sussex: Harvester Press; 1977).

Raghavan, T.C.A., *History Men: Jadunath Sarkar, G.S. Sardesai, Raghubir Sinh and Their Quest for India's Past* (Delhi: HarperCollins: 2020).

Rizvi, S.A., and Bhargava (ed.), *Freedom Struggle in Uttar Pradesh* (Lucknow: Publications Bureau: 1957; repr. Delhi: Oxford University Press: 2011).

Roy, Tapti, *The Politics of a Popular Uprising: Bundelkhand in 1857* (Delhi: Oxford University Press: 1996).

Roy, Tapti, *Raj of the Rani* (Delhi: Penguin: 2006).

Reeves, P.D. (ed.) *Sleeman in Oude* (Cambridge: Cambridge University Press: 1971).

Russell, W.H., *My Indian Mutiny Diary* (London: Cassell: 1957).

Sampath, Vikram, *Savarkar: Echoes from a Forgotten Past, 1883–1924* (Delhi: Viking: 2019).

Savarkar, *The Indian War of Independence, 1857* (London: 1909).

Sen, S.N., *1857* (Delhi: Publications Division: 1957).

Sharar, A. H., *Lucknow: the Last Phase of an Oriental Culture*, translated and edited by E.S. Harcourt and F. Hussain (Delhi: Oxford University Press: 1989).

Sinha, H.N., *The Rise of the Peshwas* (Allahabad: Indian Press Publications: 1954).

Sitaram, *From Sepoy to Subedar* ed. by James Lunt, translated by Captain Norgate (London: Routledge and Kegan Paul: 1970).

Smyth, John, *The Rebellious Rani* (London: Frederick Muller: 1966).

Srivastava, A.L., *First Two Nawabs of Oudh* (Lucknow: Upper India Publishing House: 1933).

Stokes, Eric, *The Peasant and the Raj: Studies in Agrarian Society and Peasant Rebellion in Colonial India* (Cambridge: Cambridge University Press: 1978).

Stokes, Eric, *The Peasant Armed: The Indian Rebellion of 1857* (Delhi: Oxford University Press: 1986).

Taylor, Miles, *Empress: Queen Victoria and India* (London: Yale University Press: 2018).

Taylor, P.J.O., *Companion to the Indian Mutiny of 1857* (Delhi: Oxford University Press: 1996).

Thomas, Keith, *Religion and the Decline of Magic: Studies in Popular Beliefs in Sixteenth and Seventeenth Century England* (Harmondsworth: Penguin: 1971).

NOTES

INTRODUCTION

1. Bertolt Brecht, *The Life of Galileo* (London: Methuen: 1963), Scene 13.

2. James Mill, *The History of British India* (London: J Madden: 1840), vol. I, pp. 2–3: cited in Ranajit Guha, 'Colonialism in South Asia: A Dominance without Hegemony and Its Historiography' in Ranajit Guha, *Dominance without Hegemony: History and Power in Colonial India* (Delhi: Oxford University Press: 1998), p. 77.

3. Quoted in Robert E. Sullivan, *Macaulay: The Tragedy of Power* (London: Belknap Press, Harvard University Press: 2009), p. 141.

4. Quoted in Thomas R. Metcalf, *The Aftermath of Revolt: India, 1857–1870* (Princeton: Princeton University Press: 1964), pp. 21–22.

5. This paragraph is heavily indebted to two essays by Ranajit Guha and to two essays by Partha Chatterjee. See Guha, 'Dominance without Hegemony' already cited before, from which (p. 45) the quoted words are taken; and also 'An Indian Historiography of India: Hegemonic Implications of a Nineteenth-Century Agenda' in *Dominance without Hegemony*, pp. 152–212. Also see Partha Chatterjee, 'The Nation and Its Pasts' and 'Histories and Nations' in Partha Chatterjee, *The Nation and its Fragments: Colonial and Postcolonial Histories* (Delhi: Oxford University Press: 1994).

6. Guha, 'Indian Historiography of India', p. 177; also Chatterjee, 'Nation and its Pasts'. The quoted words are cited on p. 77 of Chatterjee's essay.

7. See Partha Chatterjee, *Nationalist Thought and the Colonial World: A Derivative Discourse?* (London: Zed Books: 1986), pp. 58–59.

8. Rabindranath Tagore, 'Jhansir Rani' (originally published in the journal Bharati in 1877): *Rabindra Rachanavali* (Calcutta: Viswa Bharati: 1997), vol.30, pp. 317–22.

9. Rajanikanta Gupta, *Sipahi Juddher Itihas* (Calcutta: Bengal Medical Library: 1879-1901), 5 vols.

10. Sugata Bose, *His Majesty's Opponent: Subhas Chandra Bose and India's Struggle Against Empire* (New Delhi: Allen Lane: 2011), p. 246.

11. Jawaharlal Nehru, *The Discovery of India* (Calcutta: The Signet Press: 1946), p. 105 and p. 384.

12. Jawaharlal Nehru, *An Autobiography* (London: The Bodley Head: 1936), Chapter IX, entitled 'Wanderings Among the Kisans.'

13. S.B. Chaudhuri, *Civil Rebellion in the Indian Mutinies, 1857–1859* (Calcutta: The World Press: 1957). For an assessment of this book see Rudrangshu Mukherjee, 'Two Responses to 1857 in the Centenary Year' in Crispin Bates (ed.) *Mutiny at the Margins: New Perspectives on the Indian Uprising of 1857* (Delhi: Sage: 2014), pp. 61–71.

14. Chaudhuri, *Civil Rebellion*, pp. xxii–xxiii.

15. Chaudhuri, *Civil Rebellion*, p. v.

16. Ibid., pp. v–vi.

17. Ranajit Guha, *Elementary Aspects of Peasant Insurgency in Colonial India* (Delhi: Oxford University Press: 1983), p. 15. Also see, Ranajit Guha, 'The Prose of Counter Insurgency' in Ranajit Guha (ed.), *Subaltern Studies: Writings on South Asian History and Society*, vol. 2 (Delhi: Oxford University Press: 1983).

18. Abdul Halim Sharar, *Lucknow: The Last Phase of an Oriental Culture*, translated and edited by E.S. Harcourt and Fakhir Hussain (Delhi: Oxford University Press: 1989 repr.), p. 66.

19. The author of the line is May Sarton. I take it from the epigraph to John le Carré's novel *The Russia House* (New York: Alfred A. Knopf: 1989).

CHAPTER 1: ORIGINS

1. My account of the Meerut mutiny is based on J.A.B. Palmer's book *The Mutiny Outbreak in Meerut in 1857* (Cambridge, Cambridge University Press: 1966). Unless otherwise stated, all facts and quotations are taken from Palmer's book.

2. Hugh Gough, *Old Memories* (Edinburgh, 1897): cited in Christopher Hibbert, *The Great Mutiny: India, 1857* (Penguin: Harmondsworth, 1980), p. 85.

3. Most historians tend to trace the beginning of the revolt of 1857 to the Mangal Pandey episode that happened in Barrackpore on 29 March 1857. See Rudrangshu Mukherjee, *Mangal Pandey: Brave Martyr or Accidental Hero?* (Delhi: Penguin: 2005) for a reconstruction of the incident and the reasons for not seeing it as the starting point of the uprising.

4. Quoted in Saul David, *The Indian Mutiny: 1857* (London: Viking: 2002) p. 104. The uprising in Delhi is graphically described and analysed in William Dalrymple, *The Last Mughal: The Fall of a Dynasty, Delhi, 1857* (Delhi: Bloomsbury: 2006).

5. Henry Lawrence to Edmonstone, 29 May 1857: Inclosure 135 in No. 19, Appendix Papers relative to the Mutinies in the East Indies, p. 341, *Papers Relating to Indian Mutinies*, 3 vols (London, 1857).

6. This point was noted for the first time in Rudrangshu Mukherjee, *Awadh in Revolt:1857–58: A Study of Popular Resistance* (Delhi: Oxford University Press: 1984; repr. Permanent Black: Ranikhet: 2001; repr. Permanent Black and Ashoka University: 2019), pp. 65–66.

7. Kaye, *Sepoy War*, iii, p. 440.

8. Henry Lawrence to Canning, 3 May 1857: For. Dept. Secret Cons., 18 December 1857, No. 565; see also Forrest, *Selections*, ii, p. 8.

9. *FSUP*, ii, p. 5 and pp. 7–8.

10. *FSUP*, ii, p. 8.

11. A.L. Srivastava, *First Two Nawabs of Oudh* (Lucknow: Upper India Publishing House: 1933), pp. 78–79 dates the independent state of Awadh from the time Saadat Khan refused the imperial transfer to Malwa; also see Satish Chandra, *Parties and Politics in the Mughal Court 1707–1740* (Aligarh: Aligarh Muslim University: 1959; repr., New Delhi: People's Publishing House: 1972), p. 185. A different narrative regarding Saadat Khan's career, which does not mention his defiance of the imperial transfer to Malwa, is to be found in *North India Between Empires: Awadh, the Mughal, and the British, 1720–1801* (Berkeley, University of California Press: 1980), pp. 25ff.

12. Muzaffar Alam, *The Crisis of Empire in Mughal North India: Awadh and the Punjab 1707–1748* (Delhi; Oxford University Press: 1986); C.A. Bayly, *Rulers, Townsmen and Bazaars: North Indian Society in the Age of British Expansion* (Cambridge: Cambridge University Press: 1983).

13. Peter Reeves (ed.), *Sleeman in Oudh* (Cambridge: Cambridge University Press: 1971), p. 6.

14. Rudrangshu Mukherjee, 'Trade and Empire in Awadh, 1765–1804', in *Past and Present*, No. 94, February 1982, pp. 85–102. A different perspective is provided by Peter Marshall, 'Economic and Political Expansion: The Case of Oudh', *Modern Asian Studies* vol. 9, No. 4, pp. 465–82. The debate between Mukherjee and Marshall is available in 'Debate: Early British Imperialism in India', in *Past and Present*, No. 106, February 1985, pp. 167–73.

15. T.R. Metcalf, *Land, Landlords and the British Raj: Northern India in the Nineteenth Century* (Berkeley: University of California Press: 1979) pp. 39–40.

16. W.Crooke, 'Songs about the king of Oudh', *Indian Antiquary*, vol. XL, 1911, p. 62.

17. *Qaisar-ut Tawarikh*, p. 180: cited in G.D. Bhatnagar, 'The Annexation of Oudh', *Uttara Bharati*, vol. 3 (1956), p. 65.

18. Crooke, 'Songs About the King of Oudh'.

19. A detailed reconstruction and analysis of the Summary Settlement of 1856 is provided in Mukherjee, *Awadh in Revolt*, Chapter 2.

20. G.B. Malleson, *History of the Indian Mutiny, 1857–58*, 3 vols (London: Longmans Green &Co: 1878), i, pp. 407–8n.
21. Lawrence to Canning, 31 May 1857: For. Dept. Secret Cons, 18 December 1857, No. 575.
22. Telegram from H. Tucker to Canning, 11 July 1857: Forrest, *Selections*, p. 32.
23. Wingfield to Edmonstone, 1 July 1857: For. Secret Cons., 25 September 1857, No. 520.
24. Various accounts of the choice of Brirjis Qadr and of his coronation are available in *FSUP*, ii, pp. 77–88. The coronation is also described based on the above accounts in Rosie Llewellyn-Jones, 'Lucknow and the Royal Family of Awadh', in Rosie Llewellyn-Jones (ed.) *The Uprising of 1857* (New Delhi: Alkazi Collection of Photography in association with Mapin Publishing: 2017), pp. 140–59.
25. Ibid., p. 144.
26. Sharar, *Lucknow: Last Phase of an Oriental Culture*, p. 251.
27. In the eighteenth and in the early nineteenth centuries (till 1857), rulers of independent principalities acknowledged the suzerainty, even if nominally, of the Mughal Emperor.
28. Quoted in S.N. Sen, *1857* (Delhi: Publications Division: 1957), p. 271.
29. This brief account of the mutiny in Jhansi is based on the reconstruction in Tapti Roy, *The Politics of a Popular Uprising: Bundelkhand in 1857* (Delhi: Oxford University Press: 1994), pp. 29–31.
30. H.N. Sinha *Rise of the Peshwas* (Allahabad: The Indian Press Publications: 1954), pp. 144–45.
31. Sen, *1857*, p. 267n2.
32. Tapti Roy, *Raj of the Rani* (Delhi: Penguin: 2006), p. 25.
33. Quoted in Sen, *1857*, p. 268.
34. Quoted in Kaye, *Sepoy War*, i, p. 92.
35. My brief history of Jhansi up to the annexation is based on Sen, *1857*, pp. 267–70. It should be noted that there is no historical evidence that the rani did utter that *crie de coeur*. Sen says, 'She is reported to have declared . . .' (p. 270) but does not say reported by whom.

36. Roy, *Raj of the Rani*, p. 4.
37. D.B. Parasnis, *Jhansi Sansthanchya Maharani Lakshmibai Saheb Hyanchen* (Satara:1894), p. 27: cited in Sen *1857*, pp. 269–70.
38. Roy, *Raj of the Rani*, p. 6. Roy puts the year as 1828.
39. Sen, *1857*, p. 270.
40. Ibid., p. 269.
41. J. Smyth, *The Rebellious Rani* (London: Frederick Muller: 1966), p. 16.
42. Roy, *Raj of the Rani*, pp. 35–36.
43. Sen, *1857*, p. 270. But Tapti Roy writes that Gangadhar Rao was only 29 when he remarried. She cites no source for this very precise age for Gangadhar. See *Raj of the Rani*, p. 41.
44. Roy, *Raj of the Rani*, pp. 43–44.
45. Sen, *1857*, p. 268.
46. Quoted in *Raj of the Rani*, p. 64.
47. Ibid., p. 66.
48. My account of Lakshmibai's failed negotiations with the British government is gleaned from Roy, *Raj of the Rani*, Chapter 5.
49. Kaye, *Sepoy War*, i, pp. 91–92.
50. I take these grievances of the rani from Sen, *1857*, p. 269; and Roy, *Raj of the Rani*, pp. 81ff.
51. Kaye, *Sepoy War*, i, p. 91.
52. Quoted in Roy, *Raj of the Rani*, p. 76.
53. Ibid., pp. 32ff.
54. Translation of a Khureeta of the Ranee of Jhansee to the address of the Commr. And Agent Lieutenant Governor, Saugor Division, dated (supposed) 12 June 1857: For. Secret Consultations, 31 July 1857, No. A of 1857, Cons. No. 354.
55. Sen, *1857*, p. 278.
56. Quoted in Tapti Roy, *Politics of a Popular Uprising*, p. 109.
57. Deposition of Madar Bux, 23 March 1858: FSUP, iii, pp. 35–39.

CHAPTER 2: REBELLION

1. One testimony recorded, '*Sahib Logue* were murdered twice': *FSUP*, ii, p. 95.

2. Extract from a letter of Man Singh to Wingfield, 10 July 1857: For. Secret Cons., 25 September 1857, No. 516.
3. Neill to Canning, 10 July 1857, quoting message from Lawrence dated 30 June 1857: Forrest: *Selections*, ii, p. 31.
4. Extracts of Intelligence from Carnegie, 13 October 1857, Inclosure 30 in No. 7, *Further Papers* (no 7), p. 75, *Papers Relating to Indian Mutinies* (News of 13 October).
5. R. Strachey to Edmonstone, 25 January 1858 forwarding Carnegy's Intelligence, For. Dept., Secret Branch, 26 Feb 1858, Cons. No. 228 (News of mid-November 1857).
6. *FSUP*, ii, p. 92.
7. Ibid., p. 114.
8. Ibid., pp. 107ff.
9. *FSUP*, ii, p. 110.
10. Ibid., pp. 121ff.
11. Inglis to Sec. To Govt. Military Dept., 26 September 1857: quoted by Ball, *The Mutiny*, ii, p. 50.
12. Telegram from Lt Col. Tyler to the C-in-C., 6 August 1857: Forrest: *Selections*, ii, p. 173.
13. Ball, *The Mutiny*, ii, p. 18.
14. *FSUP*, ii, p. 58.
15. G. Bhadra, 'Four Rebels of Eighteen-Fifty-Seven' in Ranajit Guha (ed.) *Subaltern Studies IV: Writings on South Asian History and Society* (Delhi: Oxford University Press: 1985), p. 266.
16. *FSUP*, ii, p. 166.
17. Ghulam Murtaza's letter addressed to the king (undated): *FSUP*, ii, p. 137.
18. Outram to Campbell, 31 September 1857: Mutiny Papers of Outram, Havelock and Campbell.
19. Outram to Bruce, 2 October 1857: Forrest *Selections*, p. 235.
20. Ball, *The Mutiny*, ii, p. 44.
21. Inclosure 83 in No. 4, Further Papers (No. 4), p. 245, *Papers Relating to Indian Mutinies*.
22. Outram to Canning, 29 November 1857: For. Dept., Secret Cons, 16 March 1858, No. 62.
23. Translation of a letter arrived from Lucknow dated 15 February 1858: For. Dept. Political, 30 December 1859, Supplement No.

952; also available in For. Dept. Secret Cons., 26 March 1858, No. 79.

24. Carnegy's Intelligence, For. Dept., Secret Branch, 26 February 1858, Cons. No. 228 (News of 4 October 1857). The details of this mobilization in Lucknow are available in Mukherjee, *Awadh in Revolt*, p. 91.

25. On 6 November, two regiments and 200 men of the Sappers and Miners arrived; on 19 November, five Delhi regiments and six guns arrived. See Mukherjee, ibid., p. 91.

26. Carnegy's Intelligence, For. Dept., Secret Branch, 26 February 1858, Cons. No. 228 (News of 15 October).

27. Carnegy's Intelligence, For. Dept., Secret Branch, 26 February 1858, Cons. No. 228 (News of 4 November).

28. Mukherjee, *Awadh in Revolt*, pp. 93–94.

29. Carnegy's Intelligence, For. Dept., Secret Branch, 26 February 1858, Cons. No. 228 (News of 25 November 1857).

30. Mukherjee, *Awadh in Revolt*, p. 96.

31. Carnegy's Intelligence, For. Dept., Secret Branch, 26 Feb. 1858, Cons. No. 228 (News of 7 January 1858).

32. Gautam Bhadra in 'Four Rebels of Eighteen Fifty-Seven', p. 263 states that the maulavi was a member of a grandee family of Carnatic and had been educated in Hyderabad. But Bhadra does not cite any source for this nugget of information.

33. This account of the maulavi's life and career up to the battle of Chinhat is taken from the Deposition of Wazir Khan, late Sub. Asstt., Surgeon of Agra Dispensary: For. Dept. Political Proc., 30 December 1859, Suppl. No 312. This deposition is also available in *FSUP*, ii, pp. 147–49.

34. *FSUP*, ii p. 54.

35. Bhadra, 'Four Rebels of Eighteen Fifty Seven', p. 267.

36. Carnegy's Intelligence, For. Dept., Secret Branch, 26 February 1858, Cons. No. 228 (News of 7 January 1858). It is very possible that this news refers to events and developments that occurred in December 1857, as the informant was one Chandrika Pandit who had been in confinement in Lucknow for three and a half months. For the point that he staked his claims on divine

will, Couper to Edmonstone, 24 January 1858: For. Dept. Secret Cons. 26 March 1858, Cons. No. 70.

37. Couper to Edmonstone, 24 January 1858, as above.
38. Ibid.
39. This account of the Maulavi's life and career is taken from the Deposition of Wazir Khan, late Sub. Asstt., Surgeon of Agra Dispensary: For. Dept. Political Proc., 30 December 1859, Suppl. No. 312. This deposition is also available in *FSUP*, ii, pp. 147–49.
40. *FSUP*, ii, p. 139.
41. Carnegy's Intelligence, For. Dept., Secret Branch, 26 February 1858, Cons. No. 228 (News of 22 December 1857).
42. Ibid.
43. This phrase is from a letter, dated 11 March 1858, from an officer in the British force: quoted in Ball, *The Mutiny*, ii, p. 260.
44. Ibid., p. 256.
45. M. Maclagan, *Clemency Canning* (London: Macmillan:1962), pp. 174–75 argued that this was a military blunder on the part of the British generals. For a contrary view that this escape of the rebels was possible because the British army immediately after the fall of Lucknow was rendered inactive because its principal occupation became loot and plunder, and in fact, for a few days had ceased to be an army at all, see Karl Marx and Fredrich Engels, *The First War of Indian Independence* (Moscow: Foreign Language Publishing: 1967 repr.), pp. 136–37 and p. 152.
46. See Ball, *The Mutiny*, ii, pp. 282–83. Engels in 'The Revolt in India' wrote 'The capture of Lucknow does not carry with it the submission of Oudh.' Marx and Engels, *First War*, p. 149.
47. W.H. Russell, *My Indian Mutiny Diary*, ed. M. Edwardes (London: Cassell: 1957), p. 119.
48. Couper to Edmonstones, 24 January 1858: For. Dept. Secret Cons. 26 March 1858, Cons. No. 70.
49. Deposition of Wazir Khan, late Sub. Asst., Surgeon of Agra Dispensary: For. Dept. Political Proc., 30 December 1859, Suppl. No. 312. This deposition is also available in *FSUP*, ii, pp. 147–49.

50. Couper to Edmonstone, 9 December 1857: For. Dept. Secret Cons. 29 January 1858, Cons. No. 346.
51. Rana Beni Madho to Peshwa Rao Saheb: *FSUP*, ii, p. 395. This letter is not dated but most probably it was written sometime in April 1858. This is evident from the following passage: 'The battle in the Capital city has been lost and the town has been completely vacated. The King has left Lucknow and reached Bahraich.'
52. The details are available in Mukherjee, *Awadh in Revolt*, pp. 109–10.
53. Forsyth to Edmonstone, 5 June 1858: For. Dept. Secret Cons. 30 July 1858, Cons. No. 63.
54. Man Singh to Chief Commissioner, n.d. and Petition of Raja Maun Singh, 26 May 1858: For. Dept. Secret Cons. 30 July 1858, Cons. Nos. 72 and 65 respectively.
55. Forsyth to Edmonstone 3 July 1858: For. Dept. Secret Cons. 30 July 1858, Cons. No. 89.
56. A day-to-day account of the battle was prepared by a munshi in the employ of Man Singh. For Dept. Cons. 27 Aug. 1858, Cons. No. 39.
57. Forbes to Secy. To Chief Commissioner, 3 July 1858: For. Dept. Secret Cons 27 August 1858, Cons. No. 27.
58. Tiloi Raja to Barrow, 27 June 1858: For. Dept. Secret Cons. 30 July 1858, Cons. No. 91.
59. Forsyth to Edmonstone, 24 July 1858, For. Dept. Secret Cons. 27 August 1858, Cons. No. 33.
60. Forsyth to Edmonstone, 3 July 1858, For. Dept. Secret Cons. 30 July 1858, Cons. No. 89.
61. Enclosure Forsyth to Edmonstone, 14 August 1858: For. Dept. Secret Cons., 27 August 1858, Cons. No. 42.
62. Dalrymple, *The Last Mughal*, pp. 284–89, 329–32, 356–57 and p. 390.
63. Arrangement for a general attack on British troops throughout the protected country (Oudh) on 22 Suffur 1275 (1 October 1858): For. Dept. Secret Cons. 26 November 1858, Cons. No. 38.

64. C.A. Bayly, *Information and Empire: Intelligence-Gathering and Social Communication in India, 1780-1870* (Cambridge: Cambridge University Press: 1996).

65. Forsyth to Edmonstone, 11 October 1858: For. Dept. Secret Cons. 26 November 1858, Cons. No. 38.

66. Some of Beni Madho's acts of resistance are detailed in Mukherjee, *Awadh in Revolt*, pp. 107–34, especially pp. 130–31.

67. Forsyth to Edmonstone, 30 October 1858: For. Dept. Political Cons. 12 November 1858. Cons. No. 196.

68. The resistance is described in Mukherjee, *Awadh in Revolt*, pp. 127–34.

69. It is said that when the treaty of annexation was presented to Wajid Ali Shah he refused to sign it but offered his crown to Outram. The scene is poignantly recreated in Satyajit Ray's film *Shatranj ki Khiladi*.

70. Translation of kharita from Lakshmibai to Erskine (Commissioner and Agent, Saugor Division), 12 June 1857: Foreign Secret Proceedings, 31 July 1857, No 354; also available in *FSUP*, iii, pp. 65–66.

71. Translation of kharita from Erskine to Rani of Jhansi, 2 July 1857, Foreign Secret Proceedings, 31 July 1857, No. 354; also available in *FSUP*, iii, pp. 69–70.

72. *FSUP*, iii, pp. 48–57.

73. Sen, *1857*, pp. 280–81.

74. Ibid., pp. 281–82.

75. I.O.L.R. NWP Political Proceedings, P/230/77: Translation of a kharita from the rani of Jhansi to the Agent for C[entral].I[ndia], 1 January1858.

76. Sen, *1857*, p. 282n31. Sen adds the comment, 'This is not impossible, for a Union Jack, presented by the British Government to a former ruler of Jhansi, was discovered in the fort by Sir Hugh Rose's men.' It is not clear, of course, how the possession of a flag necessarily indicates that it was flown.

77. Robert Hamilton to R. Strachey, 23 January 1858: News from Bundelcund, 5 January 1858: I.O.L.R. NWP Political Proceedings, P/230/77.

78. Translation of kharita from Erskine to Rani of Jhansi, 2 July 1857, Foreign Secret Proceedings, 31 July 1857, No. 354; also available in *FSUP*, iii, pp. 69–70.

79. Quoted in Sen, *1857*, p. 279.

80. Ibid.

81. Robert Hamilton to R. Strachey, 23 January 1858: News from Bundelcund, 5 January 1858: I.O.L.R. NWP Political Proceedings, P/230/77.

82. This point about getting saltpetre from Gwalior is mentioned by Roy, *Raj of the Rani*, p. 141.

83. I.O.L.R. NWP Political Proceedings, P/230/77: Translation of a kharita from the Rani of Jhansi to the Agent for C[entral].I[ndia], 1 January 1858.

84. *FSUP*, iii, pp. 295–97.

85. I.O.L.R. NWP Political Proceedings, P/230/77: Translation of a kharita from the Rani of Jhansi to the Agent for C[entral].I[ndia], 1 January 1858.

86. Details of these will be found in Roy, *Politics of a Popular Uprising*, pp. 66–67.

87. *FSUP*, iii, pp. 227–28.

88. Ibid., pp. 292–93.

89. Ibid., pp. 296–97 (the report was dated 16 March 1858).

90. Ibid.

91. Ibid., p. 299.

92. Ibid., pp. 309–13.

93. Rose to Chief of Staff, 30 April 1858: Forrest, *Selections*, iv, pp. 20–41.

94. This was Hamilton's estimate quoted in Rose's letter (cited above): ibid., p. 42.

95. Rose to Chief of Staff, 30 April 1858: Forrest *Selections*, iv: p. 42.

96. Ibid.

97. Sen, *1857*, p. 287.

98. Rose to Chief of Staff, 30 April 1858: Forrest *Selections*, iv: pp. 47–48.

99. Rose to Chief of Staff, 30 April 1858: Forrest *Selections*, iv, p. 48.

100. Ibid., pp. 42–43.
101. Thomas Lowe, *Central India during the Rebellion of 1857 and 1858* (London: Green: Longman and Roberts: 1860) p. 236: quoted in Sen, *1857*, p. 288.
102. The description is from J.N. Sylvester, *Recollections of the Campaign in Malwa and Central India* (Bombay: Smith Taylor and Co: 1860): quoted in Sen, *1857*, p. 288n44; jewels being pocketed is noted by Lowe and quoted by Sen. The destruction of the library is also in Sen.
103. Rose to Chief of Staff, 30 April 1858: Forrest *Selections*, iv, pp. 49–50.
104. Rose to Chief of Staff, 22 June 1858: Forrest, *Selections*, iv, p. 83.
105. Rose to Chief of Staff, 24 May 1858: Forrest, *Selections*, iv, pp. 71–72.
106. Ibid., p.65.
107. Ibid., p. 71.
108. Ibid.
109. Rose to Chief of Staff, 22 June 1858: Forrest, *Selections*, iv, p. 83.
110. Ibid.
111. Ibid., p. 94.
112. M.W. Smith to The Adjutant-General, Poona Division, 25 July 1858: Forrest, *Selections*, iv, p. cxv.

CHAPTER 3: LEADERSHIP

1. Palmerston to Victoria, 18 October 1857: quoted in Miles Taylor, Empress: Queen Victoria and India (London: Yale University Press: 2018), p. 74.
2. This discussion of the proclamation is based on Ibid., pp. 79–83.
3. The full text of this Proclamation is available in *FSUP*, i, pp. 465–68. It is reproduced as an Appendix to this chapter.
4. Ball, *The Indian Mutiny*, ii, pp. 543–44.
5. This was the Enfield Rifle—so called because it was produced in Enfield—which could not be loaded without lubricating the cartridge. This lubrication was done through grease, but the end

of the cartridge had to be bitten off. Thus, the sepoys would be getting the grease on their tongues. Kaye, *Sepoy War*, i, pp. 488–89.

6. M.R. Gubbins, *An Account of the Mutinies in Oudh and the Siege of the Lucknow Residency* (London: Richard Bentley: 1858), p. 86.

7. Narrative of the emeute at Sitapur, 3 June 1857: For. Dept. Pol. Cons., 18 March 1859: Cons. No. 129.

8. Kaye, *Sepoy War*, i, p. 568.

9. Lawrence to Canning, 9 May 1857: quoted in H.B. Edwards and M. Merivale, *Life of Sir Henry Lawrence*, 2 vols. (London: Smith, Elder: 1872), ii, p. 322.

10. Kaye, *Sepoy War*, i, pp. 484–86.

11. Sitaram, *From Sepoy to Subedar*, ed., by James Lunt, translated by Capt. Norgate (London: Routledge & Kegan Paul:1970), p. 173.

12. Keith Thomas, *Religion and the Decline of Magic* (Penguin: Harmondsworth: 1973), pp. 461–62.

13. Kaye, *Sepoy War*, i, p. 485n.

14. Ranajit Guha, *Elementary Aspects of Peasant Insurgency in Colonial India* (Delhi: Oxford University Press: 1983), p. 251.

15. Ibid., pp. 257–58.

16. Kaye, *Sepoy War*, i, p. 492.

17. Ibid., pp. 491–92.

18. Guha, *Elementary Aspects*, p. 265.

19. Quoted in Kaye, *Sepoy War*, i, p. 632.

20. G.F. Harvey, Commissioner, Agra Division, 'Narrative of Events attending the outbreak of Disturbances and the Restoration of Authority in the Agra Division in 1857–58,' p. 4: *FSUP*, i, p. 392.

21. Quoted in Kaye, *Sepoy War*, i, p. 637.

22. W. Edwards, *Personal Adventures during the Indian Rebellion in Rohilkhand, Futtehghur and Oude* (London: Smith Elder & Co: 1858), pp. 15–16.

23. R.H.W. Dunlop, *Service and Adventure with the Khakee Ressallah or Meerut Volunteer Horse, During the Mutinies of 1857–58* (London: Richard Bentley: 1858), p. 15.

24. Sen, *1857*, pp. 398–401; R.C. Majumdar, *The Sepoy Mutiny and the Revolt of 1857* (Calcutta: Firma K.L. Mukhopadhyay: 1957), p. 207-10.
25. Guha, *Elementary Aspects*, p. 246.
26. Kaye, *Sepoy War*, iii, p. 56.
27. Proclamation issued under the seal of Birjis Qadr to all zamindars and inhabitants of the country of Lucknow: For. Dept. Secret Cons., 25 June 1858, Cons. No. 69.
28. Abstract Translation of an Urzee from the Rebel Camp on the part of all the rebel officers, sepoys &c to Maharaja Jang Bahadur, no date: *FSUP*, ii, pp. 603–05. Printed as Appendix B to this chapter.
29. Ball, *The Mutiny*, ii, p. 242.
30. Proclamation issued by Prince Mirza Mahomed Feroze Shah on 3 Rujib 1274 (17 February 1858): For. Dept. Secret Cons., 30 April 1858, Cons. No. 121-22.
31. Proclamation issued by Prince Mirza Mahomed Feroze Shah on 3 Rujib 1274 (17 February 1858): For. Dept. Secret Cons., 30 April 1858, Cons. No. 121-22.
32. The full text of this Proclamation is available in *FSUP*, ii, pp. 160–62. It is reproduced as Appendix C to this chapter.
33. *FSUP*, ii, pp. 150–62. Reprinted as Appendix C to this chapter.
34. Ibid., p. 150n.
35. These counter-insurgency measures are described in Rudrangshu Mukherjee, *Spectre of Violence: The 1857 Kanpur Massacres* (New Delhi: Penguin: 1998; pbk. repr. 2007), pp. 24–30.
36. Proclamation of Bahadur Shah: *FSUP*, i, pp. 453–58. Reprinted as Appendix D to this chapter.
37. Couper to Edmonstone, 1 December 1857: For. Dept. Secret Cons., 27 August 1858, Cons. No. 25.
38. Couper to Edmonstone, 9 December, 1857: For. Dept. Secret Cons., 29 January 1858, Cons. No. 346.
39. Carnegy's Newsletter (news of 19 December 1857): For. Dept. Secret Cons. 26 February 1858, Cons. No. 227.
40. Proclamation issued by Birjis Qadr for the information and guidance of his army dated 18 September 1858: For. Dept. Political Cons. 12 November 1858, Cons. No. 194.

41. Forsyth to Edmonstone, 17 July 1858: For. Dept. Secret Cons. 27 August 1858, Cons. No. 30.

42. Enclosure Forsyth to Edmonstone, 14 August 1858: For Dept. Secret Cons. 27 Aug. 1858, Cons. No. 42.

43. Rana Beni Madho's petition, 21 July 1858: *FSUP*, ii, pp. 454–55.

44. Proclamation issued under the seal of Birjis Qadr Walee of Lucknow to all zamindars and inhabitants of the country of Lucknow: For. Dept. Secret Cons. 25 June 1858, Cons. No. 69.

45. Quoted in Tapti Roy, *Politics of a Popular Uprising*, p. 109.

46. Deposition of Madar Bux, 23 March 1858: *FSUP*, iii, pp. 35–39.

47. Sen, *1857*, pp. 410–02.

48. Ray, *Raj of the Rani*, p.136 uses both the terms to describe this document.

49. *FSUP*, iii, pp. 225–27.

CHAPTER 4: AFTERLIFE

1.   Hugh Rose to M. Mansfield, 22 June 1858: Forrest, *State Papers*, iv, p. 83.

2.   P.C. Joshi, 'Folk Songs on 1857', in P.C. Joshi (ed.) *Rebellion 1857: A Symposium* (Delhi: People's Publishing House: 1957; repr. Calcutta: K.P. Bagchi: 1986; page references to the reprint), pp. 271–87.

3.   W.H. Russell, *My Indian Mutiny Diary*, ed. M. Edwardes (London: Cassell: 1957), pp. 281–82.

4.   I.O.L.R., Board's Collection, No. 191547: Revolt of the Native Army: Measures Adopted for the Punishment of Mutineers, Deserters and Rebels. 24 December 1857.

5.   Joshi, 'Folk Songs of 1857', p. 278.

6.   Hugh Rose to M. Mansfield, 22 June 1858: Forrest, *State Papers*, iv, p. 82.

7.   The songs that Crooke collected he published in *The Indian Antiquary*, vol. Xl (1911). He grouped them under the following heads: 'Songs About the King of Oudh', p. 61ff; 'Songs from Northern India Relating to the English', p. 89ff; 'Songs from Northern India', p.115ff; and 'Songs of the Mutiny', p. 123 and p. 165.

8. Crooke, 'Songs About the King of Oudh', p. 66.

9. Kaye, *Sepoy War*, iii, pp. 361–62.

10. J. Lang, *Wanderings in India and Other Sketches of Life in Hindostan* (London: Routeledge, Warne & Routledge: 1861), pp. 93–94: quoted in Sen, *1857*, p. 270.

11. Forrest, *State Papers*, iv, Introduction, p. 162. To be fair to Forrest, he did concede that 'we must bestow our tribute of admiration for the indefatigable energy and undaunted bravery she displayed, [but] we cannot forget she was answerable for a massacre of men, women and children, as revolting and deliberate as that of Cawnpore. The voices crying underneath the sod in the garden outside Jhansi were heard and the dark account demanded.' He concluded, 'To speak of her, as some have done, as the Indian Joan of Arc' is indeed a libel on the fair fame of the Maid of Orleans.'

12. Quoted in Sen, *1857*, pp. 279–80.

13. Prachi Deshpande, 'The Making of an Indian Nationalist Archive: Lakshmibai, Jhansi, and 1857', *The Journal of Asian Studies*, vol. 67, No. 3 (Aug. 2008), p. 864.

14. Quoted in Ranajit Guha, 'An Indian Historiography of India: Hegemonic Implications of a Nineteenth-Century Agenda', in Ranajit Guha, *Dominance without Hegemony: History and Power in Colonial India* (Delhi: Oxford University Press: 1998), p. 153.

15. This above paragraph is entirely based on Sumit Guha, *History and Collective Memory in South Asia, 1200–2000* (Ranikhet: Permanent Black and Ashoka University: 2019), pp. 136–41.

16. S. Guha, *History and Collective Memory*, pp. 141–42.

17. See Vikram Sampath, *Savarkar: Echoes from a Forgotten Past, 1883–1924* (Viking: Delhi: 2019), Chapters 2, 3 and 4.

18. Ibid., pp. 110–13.

19. Sampath, *Savarkar*, p. 119.

20. The original edition did not even carry Savarkar's name on the title page. It simply said, 'By an Indian Nationalist'.

21. Ibid., pp. 121–22.

22. V.D. Savarkar, *The Indian War of Independence, 1857* (London: s.n.: 1909), Introduction.

23. Ibid.
24. Ibid., p. 187n16.
25. Savarkar, *War of Independence*, p. 362.
26. Savarkar, *War of Independence*, pp. 362–63.
27. My account of Varma and his novel is heavily indebted to Deshpande, 'The Making of a Nationalist Archive', pp. 857–62.
28. See for example Roy, *Raj of the Rani*.
29. Vrindavanlal Varma, *Jhansi ki Rani* (New Delhi: Prabhat Prakashan: 1993 repr.; first published 1946), p. 179: quoted in Deshpande, 'The Making of Nationalist Archive', p. 859.
30. Varma, *Jhansi ki Rani*, pp. 116–17, 151–53: cited in Deshpande, p. 859.
31. Vrindavanlal Varma, *Jhansi ki Rani*, pp. 208–209: cited in Deshpande, p. 860.
32. Ibid., p. 338: cited in Deshpande, p. 860.
33. Varma quoted in P.C. Gupta, '1857 and Hindi Literature' in Joshi, *1857: A Symposium*, pp. 232–33.
34. Mahasweta Bhattacharjee, *Jhansir Rani* (Calcutta: New Age Publishers: 1956). All translations mine.
35. Bhattacharjee, *Jhansir Rani*, pp. 110–12.
36. The above aspects of Lakshmibai's actions are taken from Bhattacharjee, *Jhansir Rani*, pp. 131, 134–35.
37. Bhattacharjee, *Jhansir Rani*, pp. 145–46.
38. Bhattacharjee, *Jhansir Rani*, p. 327.
39. The word anthem is being used advisedly as the poem being referred to was sung by Shubha Mudgal in Parliament to mark the 150th anniversary of the uprising. Dr Manmohan Singh was the prime minister at the time. I am grateful to Ishan Chauhan, the great grandson of Subhadra Kumari Chauhan, for this information.
40. Joshi, 'Folk Songs on 1857', p. 277.
41. I take the English translation of the poem from allpoetry.com/Jhansi-ki-Rani. The English version conveys nothing of the verve, the poignancy and the inspiration of the original.
42. Savarkar, *War of Independence*, p. 260.
43. Savarkar, *War of Independence*, p. 260.
44. Savarkar, *War of Independence*, p. 260.

45. Crooke, 'Songs about the King of Oudh', *Indian Antiquary*, vol. XL (1911), p. 66.
46. Sen, *1857*, pp. 295–96.
47. It is also worth noting that there are no well-known novels about Hazrat Mahal. The essay 'Urdu Literature and the Revolt' by Ehtesham Husain in Joshi (ed.) *1857* does not mention any.
48. Partha Chatterjee, 'The Nation and its Women' in Partha Chatterjee, *The Nation and Its Fragments: Colonial and Post Colonial Histories* (Delhi: Oxford University Press: 1994), p. 131.
49. Gyanendra Pandey, *A History of Prejudice: Race, Caste, and Difference in India and the United States* (Cambridge: Cambridge University Press: 2013), p. 196.
50. Ruby Lal, *Coming of Age in Nineteenth Century India: The Girl-Child and the Art of Playfulness* (Cambridge: Cambridge University Press: 2013).
51. Ibid., p. 5.
52. These features of life in Lucknow are all described in Abdul Halim Sharar, *Lucknow: The Last Phase of an Oriental Culture*, translated and edited by E.S. Harcourt and Fakhir Hussain (Delhi: Oxford University Press: 1989 repr.). The book was originally written as a series of articles between 1913 and 1920.
53. I take this phrase from Lal, *Coming of Age* (p. 97n51), who takes it from a novel by Zora Neale Hurston, *Their Eyes were Watching God*, which was cited in Stephanie Shaw, *What a Woman Ought to Be and to Do* (Chicago and London: Chicago University Press: 1996).
54. Sen, *1857*, p. 370.
55. Sharar, *Lucknow: The Last Phase*, p. 76; also see Llewelyn-Jones, 'Lucknow and the Royal Family of Awadh' in Llewelyn-Jones, *Uprising of 1857*, p. 157.
56. Roy, *Raj of the Rani*, pp. 205–06 citing government sources dated 1860.

INDEX

Index

sepoys on 10 May 1857, 2
11th Regiment N.I., 154
Meri Jhansi nahi dungi!, 18
Metcalf, Thomas, 10
military conquest, xii
military encounter, 13
Mill, James, xii
monarch, old, 7
Mudgal, Shubha, xvii
Mughal capital, mutineers
    entered, 5
Mughal Empire, decline of, 9
Mukhopadhyay, Rajiblochan,
    xiii
muta, 14
mutinous infantry, 6
mutiny, 4
    of 1857', 118

N
Nawab Iftikhar un-Nisa Begum
    Hazrat Mahal Sahiba, 14
Nehru, Jawaharlal, xvi
Nehru, Jawaharlal, 135
Nepal Terai, rebels into, 51
Nevalkar, Raghunath Hari, 16
North India in 1857, events in, 1

O
Oh Warriors brave', 169
open rebellion, 5
Orcha gate, rebels in, 15
Oudh troops, 33
Outram, James, 31

P
Parasnis, D. B., 19

book on Lakshmibai's life
    and career, 111–12
travelled to Jhansi, 116
Pari Khanna music school, 14
Pari, Mahak, 14, 137
peasant insurgency, 82
percussion caps production, in
    Lucknow, 29
Peshwas, in eighteenth century,
    16
pre-British Hindu–Muslim
    coexistence, 96
princes of Oudh, 10
proclamation, 91
prophecy floating, 81
public works, to improve
    condition of the people of
    India, 77
pundits, spiritual belief by, 91
Pune, Spring Festival in, 115

Q
Qadr, Birjis, xviii
Qadr, Birjis, 13, 14, 29, 72
Qasim, Mir, 9
    in Bengal, 22

R
Rajabali, xiii
Raja Pratapaditya Charitra, xiii
Ramazan, 5
Rani of Jhansi regiment, xvi
Rao, Gangadhar, 17, 18
    ruled Jhansi, 25
Rao II, Baji, 16
Rao, Peshwa Baji, 16
Rao, Ramchandra, 16

Index